Merry Christmas, Nicole

Merry Christmas, Nicole

Patricia Ann Fisher

Marshalls

First Published in 1984 under the title Gingerbread Girl by
Zondervan Publishing House

First Published in the UK in 1985
by Marshall Morgan & Scott Ltd,
3 Beggarwood Lane,
Basingstoke, Hants RG23 7LP,
United Kingdom
Marshall Pickering is a subsidiary of the Zondervan
Corporation, U.S.A.

ISBN: 0 551 01244 7

Reproduced, printed and bound in Great Britain by
Hazell Watson & Viney Limited,
Member of the BPCC Group,
Aylesbury, Bucks

To Jim

Author's Note

This book is based on a true story. Names and some events have been changed to protect the privacy of the individuals involved. There are many people who helped make this book a reality, but I especially would like to thank Larry Donaldson, Pat Johnson, Brooke Sames, and my husband, Jim, for very special assistance. Also, the book would not have been written without the encouragement of foster parents who freely love the abused and neglected children who come to them and who know what loss is.

Author's...

PROLOGUE

We became foster parents in the first place because I was tired of teaching. No, that's not quite true; teaching itself was rewarding and fun. It was the other tasks that I wanted to escape: watching 200 kids drop spaghetti all over the cafeteria floor and then grind it in with scruffy shoes; enduring playground duty at 7:30 A.M. in fog so dense that neither the playground nor the children were visible; keeping records and writing detailed reports to the principal, the bilingual specialist, the reading specialist, and the specialist's specialist called the coordinator; having all the reports come back stamped "Out of compliance"; and finally, realizing that no one was ever in compliance or even knew what compliance meant. So year after year, I just taught the best I could (out of compliance, of course) and soon a decade had passed. I wanted out, maybe not permanently, but I was due for a respite. So I took a leave of absence to write a book.

"Are you really going to write a book?" David, my husband, asked.

"Of course not, that's just an excuse. What I'm really going to do is stare at that blank wall in the living room for one whole year," I responded.

That was in May. All through June I stared at the wall, interrupted only by the fact that there were five children in the house who made occasional demands on my time.

"Mom's doing it again," whispered Jill.

"How long is she going to look at that wall?" asked Julie.

Laura ordered, "Get out of here, you two. Mom is definitely not to be disturbed when she's concentrating on the wall."

"Mom, have you seen my bathing suit?" yelled Matt as he stumbled down the stairs.

So I quit staring at the wall and wrote a book on

9

everything I knew about teaching. It was quite short. That was in July and August. By mid-September I had shipped it off to a publisher and the children were back in school, so it was calm and peaceful enough for observing walls. Only now I was out of the mood. I knew every crack and crevice in the wall, but all I'd learned was that it needed to be painted. At that moment of realization, I terminated my relationship with the wall.

I began working on another book, but it was difficult to concentrate without the constant interruption of five children. "What am I going to do, David? I've looked at the wall and I've written a book and it's only September."

"I warned you: home is no place for someone who detests housekeeping and cooking," David admonished gently.

"I could write another book if only there were enough noise so I could concentrate."

"We could borrow some children," David replied. "I've always wanted to be a foster parent, you know. There are so many children that need homes. We have room for more kids and certainly enough love. And it would be practical too. They'd interrupt your concentration and then you could write."

What a great idea. After all, we had five children of our own who were healthy and happy. We were being selfish not to share our blessings.

Becoming a foster parent involved filling out papers to convince authorities we were financially solvent, had no criminal record, and were in good health. We had to have three references attesting either to our character or lack of it.

The fire marshal came out to be sure our house was safe for children. He said it was the first time he'd ever seen a smoke detector mounted directly over the kitchen stove.

"But that's where I start all the fires," I explained.

"But you need it over here by the doorway," he protested.

"Why?" I asked. "The fires start here."

I could tell he was becoming exasperated, so I showed him the other six smoke detectors (in proper places) and even let him hold the fire extinguisher for a little while.

Finally, a social worker came out. She subtracted children from beds (and for ten years I'd been telling the children "You can't subtract oranges from apples") and decided we had room for two more children.

"The children you'll get will be from Child Protective Services, a division of welfare," she explained. "They probably will have been abused or abandoned. They will have been removed from their families by the courts. Most of them will have problems, some severe. Although you'll receive a monthly check for food and clothing, you'll discover it isn't enough. Foster parents give and give and give . . . but you'll discover that yourselves."

We did . . .

CHAPTER · 1

It was Christmas Eve, a typical California Christmastime with fingers of fog pushing aside the bushes surrounding the house and cautiously peeping into the room filled with the disarray of the season. Choosing to ignore the disorderly room, I peered through fog and falling dusk to watch an approaching car. As the porch light cast an eerie welcome, the vehicle crept slowly to the curb where its engine shuddered into silence.

The car door opened and an unfamiliar figure emerged, gingerly carrying a bulky package. I opened the door quickly and greeted a rosy-cheeked replica of Santa without the fringe benefits of beard and suit.

"Hi, I'm Greg Adams and this is Nicole," he announced as the bundle in his arms began to cry. Looking around at the Christmas decor, he smiled as he handed the baby to me. "She's just in time for Christmas."

I peeled back the blanket as I took the baby whose cries were now screams. She squinted at me with terror and suspicion, her little body rigid in my arms. Speaking soothingly, I said, "It's all right, Nicole, you're home now; no one is going to hurt you." She halted in mid-scream, eyed me with all the apprehension of a six-month-old skeptic, and continued to scream with unwavering intensity.

"Well, I guess you've heard babies scream before," Mr. Adams quipped, simultaneously glancing at his watch with impatience.

"Plenty of times," I admitted, "but I've never heard such a cry of agony." I clasped the child closely, trying with little success to comfort her.

"She's still terrified," he conceded. "She weighed seven pounds at birth and only nine at the hospital just now, so she's more than a little undernourished. The bruises aren't much, at least the ones we can see. Those marks around her

13

mouth are from the grandmother's hand. Guess they really tried to turn the kid off. Both the mother and grandmother. Lucky for the kid, they have nosy neighbors. Well, thanks for taking her; I know I didn't give you much warning." Consulting his watch again, he muttered, "I gotta' go. Merry Christmas!"

"Merry Christmas," I responded weakly, but he was already closing the door.

"Well, Nicole, two pounds in six months. Either you don't like to eat or someone doesn't like to feed you." I cuddled her closely to me, but her body remained rigid and the howling persisted. *Ann,* I told myself, *you did it this time, trekked all the way to Bethlehem without benefit of the star.*

My attention was temporarily diverted from Nicole's screams as the headlights of our elderly station wagon penetrated the fog, pinpointing the driveway with practiced ease. I heard the car doors slam and the cheerful voices of my family giggling with pre-Christmas anticipation as they rushed the front door. They halted in unison in the hallway, staring and silent. *They are definitely and absolutely neither shepherds nor wisemen. Maybe sheep, though,* I pondered tentatively. Nicole, unaware of the intruders, continued to yell.

"What is that?" demanded fourteen-year-old Matt.

"This is called a baby," I explained with exaggerated patience.

"Where'd we get it? How long is it going to stay? Does it cry all the time?" asked thirteen-year-old Lisa who knew enough in a family of seven not to mince questions.

"Her name is Nicole; we'll have her as long as she needs us; and I think she *does* cry all the time."

"We leave you one hour on Christmas Eve and look what happens," lamented sixteen-year-old Laura in her eldest child's patronizing tone. "Looks like we're doing mangers this year." I didn't tell her that I'd had exactly the same thought.

14

"Here, let me take her." I could always trust David to have a practical suggestion. "I've had a little experience," he twinkled.

"Five kids is not what I'd call experience," Laura added. "Most people learn from experience." She flounced to her room. *She'll have one absolutely perfect child,* I thought. As a baby she even burped neatly. As a toddler she made perfect mud pies, and her first day of kindergarten she conquered the school system. Now we could count on her being unerring in any argument—or at least on being able to convince the others of her invincibility.

Meanwhile, experience was not helping David, so I decided on the warm bottle approach. Julie and Jill, our eight-year-old twins, followed me to the kitchen.

"So, this is what you've kept these baby bottles for," commented Jill.

Not wanting to destroy a child's illusions at Christmas, I merely smiled. There was no reason for her to know I hadn't cleaned the cupboards in eight years. Big-eyed, Jill and Julie marveled at my expertise in pouring milk from a carton to a bottle and then warming it.

Unimpressed, David yelled, "Lost the knack, honey? Hurry, this kid wants to eat. She must be starved!"

Testing a drop of milk on my arm for temperature, I handed the bottle to David. Expertly, he inserted the nipple into the baby's mouth. She sucked greedily, and David gave me his "it-takes-someone-who-knows" smile. At that moment Nicole abruptly stopped sucking and began to howl again.

"I guess I could change her," I suggested. "Lisa, get those baby clothes down from your closet."

Lisa hurried off, "Sure, Mom, they're on the closet floor; they fell down last summer when I was trying to find my swimming suit."

In spite of Nicole's continuing sobs, I smiled. Lisa was a child after my own heart. Quite obviously if the clothes had

15

fallen to the floor, that must be their rightful place. It was, as I called it, the divine right of things.

As I undressed Nicole, we all gasped at our first sight of her tiny, emaciated body. It was a mass of bruises. She shuddered from cold and pain. "Oh, Nikki," I murmured, "I'm so sorry. We won't ever let this happen again, not ever." I dressed her carefully in the softest gown, a remnant of a time long ago when people had given us gifts for having babies.

The children stood together, eyes wide with shock. Even Laura emerged from the sanctuary of her room. "I'll hold her, Mom," she offered softly.

But it was David and I who took turns holding her through that long Christmas Eve, rocking her, loving her, willing her to live. At some point in the night, Nicole reluctantly drank an ounce of milk, at another she slept for half an hour, but mostly she alternately cried, screamed, and yelled.

Just before Christmas dawned, I still held the tiny bundle and whispered lullabies. Matt tiptoed in and stood by the rocking chair. "Mom, Jesus got Christmas gifts, we have nothing for Nicole."

"Oh, yes, we do, Matt. She just doesn't know how to accept our gift yet. It's called *love*," I replied softly.

"How will she learn to accept love?"

"The way you did, Matt, and the way all the others did. You learned to love by being loved. And that's how Nicole will learn too. It will be a little harder for her, though, because she isn't sure if love is real."

And so Nicole cried, unaware of Christmas, unaware of love. She didn't know that her Christmas journey had ended, that she'd found her very own manger. And we hadn't found a way to tell her.

At near dawn, the telephone rang and David, half asleep in a chair, sat up suddenly and gasped. "The Great Aunts—I forgot them!" He dove out the door not even bothering to answer the phone.

The Great Aunts arrived every Christmas morning. Some years ago, a major airline had offered a bargain flight from Chicago to San Francisco at midnight Christmas Eve. Unable to resist a bargain, the two had been on that flight every ensuing year, even though the budget fare had long been discontinued. Needless to say, the timing of their arrival was a great inconvenience to the rest of the family.

Half an hour after David's departure, they arrived, David breathless and still apologizing, the aunts unforgiving, their faces tight with disapproval.

"David," Aunt Martha began, "informed us that you were too busy with someone's baby to pick us up." David shrugged helplessly.

Caroline, always the more practical of the two, patted her stern blue upsweep and crooned to Nicole, "Well, that's apparently our little intruder. Come to Aunt Caroline, little one."

She took the now whimpering child, and immediately Nicole started to shriek. "Heavens, what a reaction." Caroline exclaimed and she thrust the child at Martha. "Here, you take her."

"Now, why would I take a howling infant who kept me waiting in a freezing airport terminal on the day of our Lord's birth?"

Rescuing Nikki, I reached for a clean diaper. "Nicole didn't keep you waiting anywhere. It was the rest of us who forgot."

"You need another child like . . ." Martha began, then gasped, as she caught sight of Nicole's bruises. "Who beat this child?" she demanded.

"I *tried* to tell you," David muttered, knowing full well that the Aunts never listened when they could be talking instead.

"According to the social worker, she was beaten by her mother and grandmother."

"Well, they ought to be shot," Martha snapped.

"You are against capital punishment," Caroline reminded her.

Before a debate on the penal system could begin, I interrupted. "Anyone going to church?" Our five scrambled to their rooms to prepare.

Martha questioned, "Have they reupholstered those kneelers yet?"

As I shook my head she went on, "Those kneelers just weren't made for seventy-year-old knees. I thought all Episcopalians were rich—they ought to spend some of that money to fix up the church."

"Now, Martha," Caroline chided, "who yells loudest at our Episcopal Church Women's meetings that the money ought to go to missions first? Besides, my knees are just a year younger than yours. Stop talking like a cantankerous old woman."

David rose impatiently, ending the argument, "All right, all you sitting, standing, and kneeling sinners, the bus for St. Mark's is taking off in exactly two minutes." He turned to me. "I take it that you and Nicole will be holding down the fort at home."

"Yes, but remember to pray for her, David. It just seems that if God sees the little sparrow fall . . ." My voice broke.

"I'll remember," David promised as he herded the family out the door.

I looked down at the small form in the crib, which had been hastily retrieved from retirement in the attic. Nicole slept now, in complete weariness.

"Hi, little one." I touched the soft down of her hair. "You're safe now, you know." She sighed, a body-quivering sigh that spoke of weariness, both of crying and of life. "Let's have some more bottle so you can grow strong like the big kids." I caressed her face gently, then picked her up tenderly. "Softly, carefully," I told myself. She grasped the bottle greedily and drank three ounces of milk. I burped her gently and returned the nipple to her mouth. She screamed loudly. "All right, Nicole, that's enough for now, anyway. We wouldn't want an obese child." Little danger, I thought. But it's best not to push her. Let her discover love first and then all other things will come in their own time.

So Christmas Day passed with the Great Aunts commenting unfavorably on California weather, my cooking, and about a family with five children who took in a screaming sixth. At some time we did open gifts, but later I could not remember when, because no gift could surpass Nicole. Undernourished, bruised, frightened, unloved, she had been, in some unknown way, chosen for us. What greater gift could we have received?

CHAPTER · 2

With after-Christmas weariness Nicole and I visited the pediatrician's office. Holding Nicole—comfortably asleep in her newly acquired infant seat—in one arm, and purse, rattle, and diaper bag in the other, I tried to give the impression of competence. After all, I'd done this five times before, once even with twins. Nevertheless, as I signed in at the receptionist's window, I found it incredibly difficult to balance Nicole and the necessities that accompanied her. And if I remembered correctly, I had been surrounded by the same kind of amused smiles then as I was now. I sank gratefully into an empty chair and, in the process dumped the contents of my purse and the diaper bag on the floor.

A faultlessly groomed woman helped me gather the scattered items. "Your first?" she asked with a hint of amusement.

"No, the sixth," I replied, trying to sound nonchalant.

Incredulous, she turned her attention toward her own freshly bathed and powdered infant. As his name was called, she slung her purse and diaper bag casually over one shoulder and, with studied expertise, lifted the infant carrier and disappeared into the doctor's office.

I was quietly plotting a world-wide rebellion of the inept when the nurse called Nicole's name and ushered us into an examining room. I'd learned long ago, however, that this is where the waiting room actually is. In reality, it's the second-stage waiting room designed for hardy souls who survive the first. If a patient could not live long enough to survive until the second stage, the illness was undoubtably incurable anyway.

In second stage, Nicole's clothes were removed and she was weighed and measured. She shivered and cried and I did my one-person-entertainment act which, unfortunately, had never entertained any of the other five either.

On either side of me, I heard doors opening and closing indicating that either a physician or someone talented in the art of slamming doors was present. I would have settled for nearly any alternative, as Nicole cried ceaselessly and without restraint.

"Well, who is *this?*" greeted Dr. Lyons with annoying cheerfulness as he finally entered the room. He glanced at Nicole and then searched my face. "Is there an answer to the *why* I am about to ask?"

"No, except she needed us and we were there. Her name is Nicole."

He shook his head thoughtfully and began to examine Nicole with gentleness and great care. "Sure hope they got x-rays and pictures; the bruises are nearly gone now."

"X-rays! Why? This child was beaten, really *beaten* when she came to us. Doctors at emergency saw her then. And look at her weight. Besides that, she cries constantly, can't respond to cuddling and . . ."

"Hey," he interrupted gently, "I'm on her side. I'm just thinking of the courts. For now, let's put her on formula to try to bring up that weight. TLC will do the rest. You know, I used to get upset at these cases. I guess I still do." Changing the subject abruptly, he asked, "And what do the other five think of her?"

"They've survived this long in an unpredictable environment. Anyway, it's Nicole's task to win them over, and she seems to be accomplishing that successfully."

"She's certainly delayed developmentally," he observed. "Has she ever smiled? And does she turn over or anything? After all, she's six months old."

"If you'd just been beaten, you probably wouldn't lie around grinning either," I retorted. "I've been doing some baby exercises with her during her bath, but I didn't want to push things because I know she hurts all over."

"Let's see her in a couple of weeks and we'll be able to tell more about her then. I would wager this isn't the first time

22

she's been beaten, so it's hard to assess any permanent damage." As he left, he turned and smiled. "She's a lucky baby to have found a place with people who care." Suddenly businesslike again, he said, "We have to assume that she's had no shots. The nurse will be in."

Nicole stared at me, her eyes wide with terror. "It's all right, Nikki, we're almost finished, and then we can go home," I reassured her.

When the nurse entered with the needle, she spoke to Nikki gently. "It will only hurt for a minute, little one." But both Nicole and I knew that was not true—that there had been nothing but hurt for six months.

Nicole screamed and then settled down to unremitting sobs as we hurriedly left the office and began the drive home. "Lady," I began softly, "no one can cry all the time. On the other hand, we don't expect you to laugh continually either. Some laughing, some crying, and lots of talking. That's what your sibs do. You've got some catching up to do. You heard Dr. Lyons. He said you were 'developmentally delayed.' You and I both know that he's wrong, but we'll just have to prove it to him."

Nicole stopped crying and stared at me uncertainly.

"I didn't mean you had to be silent. That would really drive me up a wall. There's never been a quiet baby at our house." I glanced over at her snuggled in her car seat, eyes resting gently on me, her mouth curving into a hesitant smile.

"You did it, Nicole! A real smile! Hurray!—Except I just ran a red light watching you!" She smiled outright. "You little outlaw," I muttered with a grin.

Jill and Julie considered it their mission in life to tell everyone that Nicole could smile. Strangers would stop me at the market and say, "Oh, this is the baby that smiles. My Kate (or Susie or Jennifer) is in second grade with Julie and Jill." Then they'd smile at Nicole and she'd smile back. I'd float away with my grocery cart, forgetting half the groceries.

23

Ridiculous, I told myself. *You were worried if the others weren't crawling at her age. And you were also the one who wailed when Matt walked at nine months.* Still, I went on being unaccountably elated because the six-month-old baby at our house could smile.

Nicole's fame spread beyond the children's circle of friends and their families. One morning when I called the local high school to report that Matt was ill, I was surprised when the secretary inquired anxiously, "Well, is *Nikki* all right?"

"Nikki?"

"Oh, yes," she replied. "Matt and Laura talk about her all the time and show everyone her picture. She must be the best baby in the whole world."

"We think so," I replied, still a bit nonplussed.

Nicole and I did baby exercises every day. I'd stretch her arms to her sides, massage them gently, and then fold them over her chest. At first she watched me with apprehension and skepticism, but gradually I could feel her muscles relax and she would begin to smile and coo. Then, taking each little matchstick leg, I would help her kick until she began to take control herself, first hesitantly, then with unrestrained enthusiasm.

I retrieved last year's beach ball from Lisa's closet floor. Suspicion lurked in Nikki's eyes as I lay her backwards on the ball, arching her back over it and letting her reach for a toy on the floor with arms outstretched over her head. Rolling her sideways, my hands firmly at her waist, I could feel her underdeveloped muscles tighten. Finally, I turned her stomach down, spread eagle on the ball, and rolled her gently from side to side. Nikki smiled and cooed as I removed her from the ball and put her to my shoulder. "Nikki, you are an absolutely super baby!"

Everyone soon learned to do Nikki's exercises, but Jill and Julie became the self-proclaimed experts. One day I heard Julie instructing Jill. "Now you move this arm and leg and

I'll move the other arm and leg and then Nikki can crawl."
With an uncoordinated effort, they finally maneuvered
Nikki into a crawling position.

"Ready, go," instructed Julie.

"C'mon, Nikki," yelled Jill in encouragement.

Nikki looked from Julie to Jill, her brow furrowed in
bewilderment.

As the twins moved her arms and legs with a totally
awkward effort, Nikki collapsed in a heap and burst into a
rusty little giggle.

"Mom, Mom, she laughs!" yelled Jill proudly as she too
burst into giggles, followed somewhat reluctantly by Julie,
whose original project had been an unequivocal failure.

Leaving the threesome giggling, I marveled at the triumph
of laughter, how the little voice which could once express
only fear and pain could now echo with happiness and love.

Nikki became an accomplished giggler. Nearly everything
provoked an eruption of giggles. David noted that she may
have been making some kind of profound commentary on
our family.

Matt appointed himself chief verbal instructor and took
his turn as exerciser as well. Say "Mama," he'd coax. Nikki
would merely giggle in response. "Stop giggling," he commanded sternly. "You don't want to be known as 'Nikki, the
giggler,' do you?" Nikki giggled.

I watched Matt rolling over and over on the floor and
Nikki following him with effort and concentration. My eyes
misted as I remembered the very first thing I had heard
about Matt on the day he was born. The stiffly starched night
nurse had come in smiling. "Can't sleep?" she inquired.
"Your son has the same problem. He keeps turning over.
We don't seem to be able to convince him that newborns
don't do that." Certainly Matt was the perfect one to teach
Nikki what he himself had known by instinct.

There was always another sibling waiting to go on stage as
Nikki's teacher. One day as Lisa held Nikki above her head

she commented, "Good, Nikki, arms and legs out straight like an airplane. Here comes Nikki, the airplane," she announced as she and Nikki circled the living room. Finally, exhausted, they collapsed in the rocker. "Hey, Mom, is that really an exercise or is it a game?" And I knew we'd won, that we'd integrated learning and living.

I was so engrossed in Nikki's progress, I nearly forgot there should be others involved, so it was two months before I made our next appointment with Dr. Lyons. At eight months she was a happy, gurgling baby, but it was time for the next series of DPT and polio shots.

I entered the doctor's office triumphantly, carrying Nikki with complete confidence. As Nikki held out her arms to him, Dr. Lyons smiled broadly. "I just can't believe this is the same child. She's gained five pounds and it looks like its all pure love!"

"We *are* pleased with her weight gain; she certainly loves to eat. And she's doing so well trying to crawl. But I'm worried about speech patterns. All the other children could say at least two or three words at her age."

"Well, you can't expect her to get her act together all at once." As Nikki smiled at him, he picked her up and hugged her. "See how social she is?"

Nikki's timing couldn't have been more exact. "Mama, Mama," she cried, holding out her arms to me triumphantly.

"There you go," Dr. Lyons grinned. "She was just waiting for an audience."

As if she ever lacks one, I thought.

And so it was that Nikki began a word collection. When David drove into the driveway, she'd smile and yell, "Dada." The new game was "Nikki, say kitty," or "Nikki, say doggie." It went on and on, but for a long time her favorite word was "Mama."

CHAPTER · 3

The phone rang. With three teenagers in the house, that is a singularly insignificant statement because the phone is never for me. Friends have long since learned to send mailgrams or to call before six A.M. But this time Lisa yelled somewhat incredulously and more than a little indignantly, "It's for you, Mom!"

"Hello?" I answered speculatively, still suspecting that a mistake had been made.

"Hi, this is Greg Adams, Nicole's caseworker. Sorry I haven't been in touch before, but I thought you might want to know the results of the grandmother's and mother's criminal hearing."

"I didn't even know there had been one," I replied.

"Well, they were found not guilty," he said cautiously.

"Not guilty! How could that possibly be? She was covered with bruises." Suddenly suspicious, I asked, "What about the pictures of the bruises and those x-rays?"

"Well," he began apologetically. "You remember it was Christmas Eve. Everyone wanted to go home and Nicole wasn't in any life-threatening situation once we'd removed her from the home. So the x-rays and the pictures sort of didn't get taken."

"Sort of didn't get taken," I repeated. "What does that mean? Either they did or they didn't."

"They didn't," he admitted. "Frankly, the county didn't have its case prepared. We were left flat-footed at the trial. Then the grandmother and mother hired this shyster lawyer who has a vendetta against the welfare department. He thinks natural parents have an innate right to treat children in any way that seems appropriate and that includes abuse."

"The grandmother and mother just got off then?"

"From the criminal charge, yes. But now we have a jurisdictional hearing in Juvenile Court to decide if the child should remain under care or be returned to the family. And I am going to get the DA on the stick for that one. That hearing will be Thursday," he explained.

Totally baffled and disturbed, I pressed, "Greg, I don't understand any of this. I don't see how the relatives could be innocent of criminal charges when the bruises and neglect were more than apparent. And it is totally inconceivable to me that the courts could even consider returning the child to that environment."

"We'll do our best," he replied. "See you." He hung up leaving me with at least eight more questions which probably didn't have answers either.

I sat down by the sleeping Nicole. Her hair was coming in dark brown and curly, a perfect match for her big brown eyes fringed with curly lashes. Every day now was a day to conquer new skills, to make new claims to love. Now with one, single, careless decision, would the courts condemn her to moments without learning and life without love? I had always thought that courts and welfare agencies presented all the evidence and then acted in the best interests of the child. I had much to learn.

On Thursday, the hearing day, David stayed home from work, and he and I and Nicole went to the zoo. It was one of those unpredictable, springlike days that the end of February sometimes offers as a reprieve from winter. It also might be the last day we had with Nicole.

As we wandered aimlessly around the zoo, Nicole, bundled in her fuzzy, pink snowsuit, stared wonderingly at the animals. David and I absently tossed popcorn at them and stared wonderingly at Nicole.

"How long do hearings last?" I asked David.

He shrugged. "They aren't going to return Nicole to that home. It's not even reasonable, logical, justifiable—need any more words?"

"No, but if you're so certain of the outcome, why did you stay home?"

"I had a longing to see the zoo," he replied. But we both

knew we were searching for some way to say goodbye to a small child, unwilling to admit that there was no way.

"It's three o'clock. I heard someone say that judges begin work late, quit early, and do very little in between. Maybe Nikki's case was heard in that 'in between' time," I suggested.

"I guess we could call," David suggested.

We both knew we were nearing an end to a flight from reality, a day of pink balloons, cotton candy, popcorn, and zoos. Reluctantly we found the nearest public phone. David dialed as we both studied Nicole intently. "Greg Adams, please." David spoke in a business-like tone.

"What's he saying?" I asked anxiously.

David covered the mouthpiece with his hand and turned to me with a pretense of annoyance. "He said, 'Hello,' and if you're quiet enough I'll have some hope of hearing the rest."

The rest was that the court had found the grandmother and mother currently incapable of caring for the child, that a plan of reunification had been approved, and that the child would remain in foster care in her present home for one full year.

David explained to me that the plan of reunification would include bi-monthly visits by the grandmother and mother and that both would be required to attend mental health therapy on a weekly basis.

Another year with Nicole! We still held the pink balloon, refusing to believe that it would ever burst.

The day of the first visit with Nicole's relatives, I dressed her in a lace-trimmed pink hand-smocked dress sent by the Great Aunts from Barbados. David had commented wryly when the package arrived that the Aunts had probably found another bargain flight and had descended without notice on the island. Periodic hurricanes where the worst thing the island had had to contend with before the arrival of the Great Aunts. As a result of their trip, Nicole was outfitted with a whole wardrobe of hand-smocked dresses in every conceivable hue and design. Now dressed in one of them, Nicole was eager to go "bye-bye."

But as I dressed for the dreaded occasion, my own heart was heavy. Although Greg Adams had assured me that the visits would be supervised, he was strangely evasive when I'd pressed for details. Even with persistence, I was given only the most sketchy information: the meetings were to be held in a special room at the welfare department every other Tuesday and would last for an hour.

Holding Nicole securely, I entered the building labeled "Social Services" and approached the desk uncertainly. "Mr Adams, please, " I asked.

"Oh, I'm sorry," a pleasant receptionist greeted me. "Mr. Adams isn't here today."

The coward, I thought.

Flipping through some cards in front of her, she pulled one. "We do have a welfare aide to supervise the visit in room 118. That's right down the hall."

Following her directions, I opened the door to room 118 and found it already occupied. A middle-aged woman, dumpy and unkempt, waddled toward us, reaching chubby arms for Nicole. Nikki stiffened, then clung to me screaming, "Mama! Mama!" Another woman, a twenty-year-old replica of the elder, slouched in the background, filing her fingernails. The welfare aide stepped forward and removed Nikki from my arms.

"She'll be out in an hour," she announced to me with crisp dismissal.

Closing a door had never been harder. Nikki's screams penetrated the metal slab as if it were nonexistent. Somehow I relinquished her and dragged myself down the hallway.

I sat in the waiting room trying to interest myself in the people around me, then in the bestseller in my purse, and finally in the movement of the watch on my wrist. Every minute was sixty agonies.

Finally, the welfare aide emerged with a naked, screaming Nikki. "What happened?" I demanded, my heart doing the high hurdles.

"Oh, nothing," she replied indifferently. "You can dress

her back in the room. Parents often like to make certain that their child has no bruises."

I grabbed the sobbing, shivering child and headed for room 118. Quickly I dressed her in diapers and undershirt and then reached for her pink, fluffy dress. It looked like someone had wiped chocolate-covered hands on it and then had torn it like a rag. I stifled a sob for Nikki, for me, and even for the Great Aunts.

"It's all right, Nikki; it's all right." I held her close. Tucking her into her snowsuit, I hurried from the wind-cooled room.

Nikki was still screaming as we drove home. I honked the horn at little old ladies in my path, at a man in a wheelchair, and even at a red light. Reaching for the pack of cigarettes on the dashboard, I began to light one, then remembered I didn't smoke. I was ready to join any radical group, but no one seemed to be picketing anywhere.

By the time I reached home Nikki was still screaming. Until one has heard the scream of an abused child, one has not really heard a child cry. It has a terror-stricken, agony-laden, less-than-human sound. It is a cry for help and, at the same time, a rejection of it. It is a primal cry for survival in an alien world.

Lisa wheeled her bike into the driveway just ahead of the station wagon. Turning toward us, she grasped the situation at once and gently removed Nikki from her car seat. Ignoring the screams, she announced cheerfully, "Nikki, what about a warm bath with rubber ducky?" Rubber ducky had great prestige among Nikki's toys. As the two entered the house, I sat in the car for a moment regaining my own composure and feeling grateful toward my daughter, age thirteen-going-on-thirty. Despairing of a world that thought so little of children that abuse was heaped upon abuse, I cried until David came out to remind me that it was warm inside.

CHAPTER · 4

A warm bath and a rubber ducky did nothing to alleviate Nicole's screams. She wanted all of us at once and, at the same time, none of us. She went from Lisa to Laura to Matt to the twins to David to me, seemingly searching for an unknown haven and not finding it.

"David, this is the same kind of screaming that we heard those first days," I recalled. He nodded in agreement. "I wonder if all abused children sound this way?"

But Nicole herself took command of the conversation, seeming to resent any intrusion into her own story of terror which she continued with vehement, soul-baring sobs.

We took turns holding her as we had on that first night. But something had changed. We were no longer trying to comfort a stranger who had come to us because there was no place else to go. This screaming, alienated child, in some way, belonged. This child was a part of me, of David, and of the other children. And we were a part of her. I had the feeling, furthermore, that neither time nor circumstance would change that fact.

Eventually, exhaustion prevailed and when David took Nicole, I fell into a deep headache-inducing sleep, only to have him awaken me a short time later.

"Ann, Ann." David was shaking gently. "It's Nicole. She seems very ill." Foggy-minded, I roused myself and took the still screaming child.

"About 104 degrees, I'd guess," I muttered still half asleep. Nicole was burning with fever and I'd long given up on thermometers that mysteriously bounce to the floor and break at the precise moment when they are most needed. Resting my head against her chest, I could hear a deep rattle. "I've never been able to tell if its bronchitis or pneumonia," I said half apologetically to David. "I'll call Dr. Lyons."

"No, I'll call him," David announced firmly. "He's going

to see this child right now. I don't care if it is 3 A.M., I'm not going to be put off by some unintelligible answering service."

With that statement, David strode to the kitchen to dial. Minutes later he returned, looking somewhat chagrined. "I just mentioned my name and who I was calling about and Dr. Lyons said he'd meet us in emergency in ten minutes. Never even got to use my arguments."

I grabbed my coat, put a light blanket around Nicole who was generating her own body heat, and followed David to the car. On the way to the hospital, I thought about how many times we'd made that journey with a sick child and how long ago that was, perhaps even an entire lifetime ago. And in that earlier lifetime it had been amazingly easier to be up all night, I thought ruefully.

The emergency room had not changed from those earlier years. The same diverse group of people sat together, yet each alone in private worlds—a family with an indeterminate number of children accompanied a grandmother who discussed her problems in fluent Spanish, while an ancient, sleeping derelict slouched next to her. Beyond them were a neatly dressed elderly couple, the woman carefully protecting an injured arm, the man speaking in comforting tones. I took the nearest chair, holding the now-sleeping Nicole close to me, and prepared for a long wait.

"I'm here; come on back." Sounding incredibly buoyant, Dr. Lyons smiled as he peeked through the receptionist's window and motioned us back to the examining rooms.

Taking Nicole, who had started screaming again, into an examining room, I began to undress her as I heard David outlining the day's events to Dr. Lyons. My hands were strangely uncooperative as I unsnapped Nicole's terry suit and my arms shook from the exhaustion of the long hours of holding her.

A competent-looking nurse was already taking Nicole's temperature. "You know, I hate these cases," she said.

"They only end one way, in the death of the child. It's like a dead-end maze and once the child enters it, there's no way out. You need to begin to deal with that." She spoke sharply.

I couldn't answer—surely she was just a hard-bitten night emergency nurse who had seen more heartbreak than the world should require of any one person.

Dr. Lyons was back, stethescope pressed to Nicole's chest. "Pneumonia," he nodded. "Her temperature is 104 degrees on the nose." Looking momentarily amused, he said, "I certainly wouldn't invest in a thermometer when you can be that accurate without one." Then he sat somewhat precariously at the table's edge and picked up Nicole who now alternately screamed hoarsely and coughed. "Of course, I'll call about this and write a follow-up letter, but you should know that probably nothing will be done. You remember that I asked you the first time I saw her why you took this child."

"I remember. I said I didn't know. I guess there's still no reason other than she needed us," I replied.

"She still *does* need you. But do *you* need the heartbreak that inevitably accompanies these situations? Just remember that the courts will rule for the natural parent in the face of all evidence to the contrary. We can cure the pneumonia, perhaps control the screams, but we can't change a society that really places very little value on the best interests of the child."

· · ● · ·

At 8:10 A.M. I called Greg Adams. "Hi, I've been expecting your call," he announced. "Ben Lyons chewed me out royally at about 4 o'clock this morning."

35

"So what are you going to do about it?" I asked quietly, trying to control my rage.

"What I'd like to do is to tell the old lady and her daughter to get lost. And," he added, "if this phone is bugged, I've just lost my job. But to answer your question, the only thing I can do is to supervise the visit myself."

"Well, will you do that," I asked, "or continue to be a coward and be out of the office again?"

He chuckled. "You are making me rise to the occasion, aren't you? All right, I will personally sit right outside the door the entire visit. I'll instruct the relatives not to undress the baby or open the windows. Does that satisfy you?"

"But what about Nicole's reactions? Don't her feelings count at all? She's really afraid of those people."

"That's called 'primitive memory' by psychologists and there's lots of debate about whether kids can remember trauma which occurs at an early age."

"Debate? I thought that was an accepted theory way back in the days when I was in college."

"You have to be able to prove it in court and *that's* something else. Psychologists usually waffle under pressure. And judges don't like to listen to psychologists or any other expert witnesses. In fact, most judges have their own pre-conceived bias in favor of the birth parent," he added. "And, if this line *is* bugged, I'm really on my way to unemployment."

I replaced the telephone thoughtfully. Was Greg really concerned about his job? I'd heard that he was one of the better workers and yet he'd done very little to supervise Nicole. Or had he? Maybe just letting her have the experience of growing in a normal environment was enough. Or were we all setting ourselves up for some unknown looming disaster?

• • ● • •

On the following Tuesday I dressed Nicole in a warm playsuit. Her dark eyes were wide with fear and misgiving. She seemed to sense that getting ready to go "bye-bye" might not be the pleasant experience she had always known it to be in the past. "Cheer up, Nikki," I told her, "Mr. Adams put you with us in the first place so we know he has some sense." *But*, I asked myself, *would he or could he stand up to pressure?*

Now an old hand at the welfare game, I walked into the agency attempting valiantly to convince myself that all would be well. Nikki did not share my confidence, however. She looked around as solemnly as if she were staring at a spoonful of carrots with the rest of the jar waiting on her tray.

We proceeded directly to room 118 where Greg stood waiting outside the door. "I'll take her in," he said. "That way you won't have to see them." Nikki went to him reluctantly, her eyes filled with uncertainty.

As they entered the room I heard Nicole's first scream of totally unrestrained agony. I leaned against the wall outside, listening to her moan and whine like a beaten animal. Suddenly, there was a piercing scream that sounded alien and totally subhuman. I clung to the wall, hoping against hope, praying against prayer.

As if in answer, Greg, ashen-faced, emerged with Nicole and handed her to me. "I couldn't do it," he said shaking his head. "Lord knows what will happen, but I'm calling off the visit. All those social work professors who talk about reunification of child and parent haven't been through this. Just take her and get out of here," he commanded.

Again I left the building with a screeching Nicole and hurried toward the car as if being pursued by the KGB. Dumping Nikki unceremoniously into the car seat, I drove off in reverse, nearly colliding with a car parked behind me. Shifting gears, I debated the feasibility of acquiring a vice of some kind.

We all remember the following days as an uphill climb through dense fog. Except for small lulls for a gulped bottle and moments when exhaustion overcame her terror, Nicole screamed steadily for the next three days and the nights they merged with. And while Nikki fought her own nightmares, the rest of the family groped through life until every nerve was frayed.

"That's my orange juice," screamed Laura.

"How could it be? I just poured it," responded Lisa. I picked up the disputed glass and drained it.

"Mom, how could you?" they responded, united in outrage.

"It was really *my* orange juice," I replied, attempting to mimic their voices, adding my own caustic overtones. They both stared at me attempting to interrupt my comment. As I burst into uninhibited, near-hysterical laughter, they joined me, breaking the tension of the past days.

• • • •

"How will we get through another visit, David?" I asked as I observed Nicole gradually returning to smiles and giggles and baby words. "I can't remember being more fatigued. It's a combination of both emotional and physical fatigue that challenges the very act of living."

"I know, and I'm certain Greg will try to stop the visits if it's at all possible," David added, hand rubbing his forehead wearily. "And if he can't stop the visits, he ought to move in and take his four-hour shift of screaming. After all, all is fair in war and welfare, especially when they're combined," he added cynically.

But it was Greg who called us. "I went out to visit Nicole's relatives and they are gone—moved. Mental Health says they came there just one time, so as long as I don't hear from them, visits are cancelled. I have better things to do than play detective."

A new phase of the game had begun. It was called watching the calendar and willing the phone not to ring. Tuesday after Tuesday passed and the phone remained silent. And in the midst of waiting, Easter came.

CHAPTER · 5

Long before Nikki, we had made Easter and Easter Basket Day separate holidays for both theological and practical reasons. It began the year Laura was feisty four; Matt, terrible two; and Lisa, a whirlwind one. The Great Aunts had sent white organdy dresses, billowing with full slips and ruffles for the girls, and a white pique three-piece suit for Matt.

"David, they're beautiful," I remarked as I held the small garments lovingly.

"Just wait until they get decorated with chocolate bunnies," David predicted. "Presto! Self-destructing clothes."

The problem of how to reconcile chocolate bunnies and the image of three Easter angels was something only a mother would consider serious. David refused to even discuss it.

At 2 A.M. one morning the solution finally came. "David, David, wake up! I know what to do about the chocolate bunnies."

"What chocolate bunnies?" David had hurled himself from bed ready to meet the intruders. "Where are they?" he demanded, as though expecting to be assaulted by a warren of rabbits.

"Oh, David," I muttered hopelessly, "get back into bed. The chocolate bunnies that are going to ruin the children's clothes on Easter."

He sat down on the bed and glowered at me. "You woke me up at 2 A.M. to talk about the kids getting chocolate on their clothes? This had better be good," he threatened.

"It's the perfect solution. First of all, we color eggs and have our Easter egg hunt and everything on Saturday. That's Easter Basket Day. Then on Sunday—that's Easter—I dress up the kids and we go to church. Besides it's even theologically sound, I think. We get the commercial junk out of the way Saturday and then the children will grow up thinking of Easter as the religious holiday it's meant to be."

By then David was snoring.

But that's how we had done it, although for many years, other children in the neighborhood had difficulty understanding why the Johnston's Easter Rabbit came a day early.

On Easter morning, however, the Johnston children always looked angelic, and they grew up greeting each other on Easter with "He is risen" to which the next child would reply, "He is risen indeed!"

On Easter Basket Day this year all six arose early to search for Easter baskets. Laura had proclaimed that she was too old, but then had decided it would be nice to have an Easter basket filled with tennis balls and maybe one really nice chocolate egg. Lisa had declared that she always wanted an Easter basket even when she had children of her own.

But it was Nikki, clutching a blue, stuffed bunny, her mouth crammed with gumdrops, her pajamas fingerpainted with chocolate, who crawled into bed with David and me.

"Does the bunny sing?" David asked. Nikki nodded, and David wound up the musical bunny for Nikki who giggled with delight. "Let's go color some eggs, Nikki," he suggested. "The Easter bunny can't do it all by himself."

On Easter day we dressed Nikki in a new strawberry pink dress layered with white lace. Clutching her singing bunny, she bounced enthusiastically whenever one of other children said "He is risen" to her.

Lisa, trying to correct her, said, "No, Nikki, when someone says "He is risen," you say, "He is risen indeed. Now let's try it. He is risen."

Nikki, eyes sparkling, responded, "Deed, deed, deed."

In years to come, the single word 'Indeed' would say it all, but we did not yet know that.

42

CHAPTER · 6

Summer was one of California's better performances that year, bright and warm with promise. One morning, David and I sat contentedly watching Nicole scoop cereal in the general vicinity of her mouth while we drank our morning coffee.

"It's Nicole's first birthday next week. Let's take her to the coast. The rest of us could certainly use a vacation, too," David suggested.

"We certainly could," I agreed, "but I wonder if we can take Nicole out of the county?"

"I'll find out right now," David asserted as he reached for the phone. "Greg Adams, please." I listened hopefully to David's end of the conversation. "She's fine. We'd like to go to the coast for a week and were wondering if we could take Nicole." He laughed. "Yeah, I guess it would be abandonment if we left her." He paused. "The California coast, of course. Oh, you think South America might be more appropriate?" he chuckled then reluctantly asked the perpetual question: "Are the relatives still gone? Good—don't try too hard to find them." We had our approval; the trip was on.

Packing for a family of eight is enough to make any mother wish she'd never heard the word *vacation*. I remembered the time we all accompanied David on a business trip and I hadn't packed a single shirt for him. When I suggested he just wear a tie on a string around his neck with his jacket, he became quite unreasonably incensed. I laughed hysterically while he paced the floor, angrily refusing to see any humor at all in the situation. After that he did his own packing. And the others, I noticed, always checked the clothes I was packing too. Unfortunately, this meant that someone was always unpacking while I packed. This questionable method also led to such debacles as having all our dirty underwear spill in front of customs at Los Angeles International Airport following a jaunt to Mexico. I could hardly have been more mortified than if I'd been caught with a cache of marijuana. Now, Nicole, caught in the spirit of packing, crawled to the suitcase dropping in her own little treasures: half a cracker, a plastic cup, one outgrown shoe, and a handful of cat food.

I picked her up. "Oh, Nikki, what did we ever do before we had you?" She giggled and hugged me. Through Nikki I had experienced a new awareness of the world, one I had not known with the others. There used to be so much energy to rush with. Now each day was a new insight into life, a special gift. And I kept the gifts and stored the memories.

· · ● · ·

Some families probably move beyond the "when-will-we-get-there" stage, but ours never had. The twins have been known to ask on the way to the market. David now suggested that a more appropriate question might be, "*Will* we get there," considering our ancient station wagon.

The twins entertained Nicole by pointing out the sights. "Cow, Nikki. Say 'Cow'."

Nikki would obediently point "ow" and her gurgling little laugh would lead the rest of us.

"Doggie, doggie." Nikki pointed excitedly.

Jill giggled. "That's a horse, Nikki."

"Doggie," asserted Nikki with slight indignation and complete self-assurance.

Finally, Nikki's lashes rested on her cheeks and her head nodded, and she fell asleep, head thrown back and mouth wide open, completely exhausted by futile attempts to educate her stubborn siblings.

Some years ago we'd found a special place on the coast, a

place we called "ours" even though someone surely stayed there when we did not. We were convinced, of course, that the cottage accepted these intruders with great reluctance and was most certainly unwilling to part with any of the treasured moments we had spent there.

Now as we set up Nicole's portacrib, the white curtains, bolstered by the sea breeze, bristled and waved with new importance. The small rooms came alive with children's voices, suitcases opening, and challenges of, "I'll race you to the beach!"

Nicole dredged out the cracker she had packed and gazed around solemnly. "Nicole, this is a smiling house. It likes babies and children and sand on the floor and sea breezes through the open door. You'll like it here, I promise." She reached out her arms to be picked up.

"I get to show Nikki the ocean first," David announced, grabbing Nikki from me.

"No, I do," yelled Matt.

Suddenly we were all racing for the beach, not one of us wanting to miss that special moment. Nicole, laughing from David's shoulder, watched us follow with undisguised glee.

Nicole turned out to be as much of a sand dabbler as the rest of the family. She'd crawl to the exact place where sea met sand and laugh heartily as a wave would challenge her, set her sprawling, then retreat for a new attack. When tired by the relentless sea, she filled her sandpail with sand and triumphantly dumped it into the sea. "There," she'd announce with the conviction of accomplishment and then begin to fill her little sand pail again.

Finally, exhausted by wind and sea and the triumph of challenging them, she climbed onto my lap, head resting on my shoulder. She and I returned to the cottage alone for a bath, a dinner, and a time together in the chintz-covered rocking chair. Nikki patted my cheek and settled into my arms, sleep beginning to claim her.

"I love you, Nikki," I said as tears ran down my cheeks.

45

"No matter what, there's always love," I assured her, but a sudden burden had settled over me. I brushed Nikki's bangs out of her eyes and put the sleeping baby in her crib where she was watched over by sea and wind and, most certainly, by God.

· · **●** · ·

Just as the splintery fingers of dawn reached into the cottage the next morning, I heard Nicole yelling, "Mama, Mama." She certainly wasn't going to miss many moments of her special day. I slipped out of bed quietly so as not to awaken David. Quickly I donned jeans and a sweatshirt. Lifting Nikki from her crib, I planted a birthday kiss on her forehead, zipped her blanket sleeper, and quietly opened the cottage door.

"See the beach, Nikki? Remember all the fun you had yesterday?" I asked her. Her eyes danced gaily in reply. I carried her down the dewy path, slipping, more than walking, to the beach below.

"Look at the waves, Nikki. They are like love must be; there is no turning back; there's always another wave. And the ripples just dance off in every direction until no one can tell where their destination will be." Nikki looked at me somberly. "Happy Birthday, Nikki. May I have a birthday kiss?" She kissed my cheek and then took my hand in hers.

"You think you're ready to walk, huh?" I asked her. Holding her by both hands, I led her toward the ocean. When I let go, she stood alone, then took one step and then another. She stopped and looked back, grinned mischievously and took yet another step. Then suddenly she was down on her hands and knees, crawling rapidly toward the water. I caught her, and as I tucked her under my arm I said, "You know what? You're the Gingerbread Girl."

You ran away from Mama.
You ran away from Dad.
And Laura
And Matthew
And Lisa, too,
And no one can catch you,
Not even Julie or Jill,
Because you're our own little Gingerbread Girl.

The words were out and the moment broken. All at once, I didn't like the story at all because I remembered the way it ended.

"No fair having birthdays alone," David yelled as he, too, slipped down the path, miraculously balancing two coffee cups. Nicole's bottle protruded from his pocket.

"You missed it, David. She walked!"

"Didn't miss anything," he grinned. "I saw her take off while I was waiting for the coffee." He sat down on the sand, picked Nikki up and handed her the bottle. "Happy Birthday, little one," he spoke softly. Nikki took the bottle eagerly and settled blissfully onto David's lap as David and I sipped our coffee.

"David, something happened a few minutes ago that I wish never had," I commented thoughtfully.

"What, Nikki walking?" he asked.

"No, we knew she was ready to walk and it certainly is time. But you know how I made up silly rhymes from stories and nursery rhymes for the other kids?"

"Yeah, they loved them." He eyed me quizzically.

"Well, I didn't like this one and somehow it won't go away. It's just like I said it and that makes it true."

"Well, out with it and we'll exorcize this awful demon." David waved his coffee cup dramatically.

"You're sure you want to hear it?"

"Probably not." He grinned and tossed a handful of sand at me. "But it sounds like I'd better."

"It goes like this," I began.

> You ran way from Mama.
> You ran away from Dad.
> And Laura
> And Matthew
> And Lisa, too.
> And no one can catch you,
> Not even Julie or Jill,
> Because you're our own little Gingerbread Girl.

David was silent for a moment. "Just shows you shouldn't mess with poetry before coffee. Still, it does get to you," he admitted. "But," he said with determination, "this is a day for a party."

We trekked up the hill, David and I and Nicole, to the stack of gaily wrapped presents, to the new, hand-smocked dresses from the Great Aunts, to the stuffed elephant and the pull toys and the books and the blocks and the birthday cake.

The other children roared with approval as Nikki dismantled her birthday cake and stuffed fistfuls of frosting into her mouth. I laughed out loud too, but in the silence of my heart I whispered, "Happy Birthday, Gingerbread Girl."

CHAPTER · 7

As the summer grows warm, leafy green trees speak in whispers to the blue, cloudless sky, exchanging philosophies and confiding secrets. The sun smiling benignly, awakens morning glories and yawning kittens and Nicole. I hear her gurgles and know she is sharing her contentment with the trees and flowers and birds and sky and that they are all listening with approval.

As cooing gives way to hunger, I hear Nicole pull herself to a standing position in her crib, give her busy box ball a twirl, and ask expectantly, "Dinner?"

Nicole calls all meals "dinner," and although each child had patiently attempted to teach her the difference, she would only listen with bemused indifference or pretended concentration and then calmly reject the irrelevant distinction between meals.

As David buried his head under his pillow in search of more sleep, I reached for my robe, tossed my pillow at him, and turned off the alarm. Moments later, Nikki and I headed for the kitchen to prepare dinner. Secretly I shared her total disregard for labeling meals. They all produce dirty dishes.

I do not regard preparing breakfast as a rational act, and most people who have eaten my breakfasts will attest to that. Actually, my first lucid action of the day is to stroll to the driveway to collect the *L.A. Times*. But when David is first up, I have been known to remark, "Unless the *Times* is there, how do I know for sure that there is still a world and that we are going to have a day today?" So David, good-naturedly, will trudge to the driveway, get the paper, and toss it at me in bed.

"Headline reads, '*Times* Declares Tuesday,'" he will pretend to quote, and I will reluctantly abandon sleep.

But on this particular day Nikki and I got the paper. She snuggled onto my shoulder as we stopped to pick a dandelion and to decide if Nikki liked butter. We admired the profusion of morning glories, and Nikki pointed to their brightly-colored faces and commented, "Pretty." Then we returned to the house, knowing that Matt would soon arrive with the daily local which he faithfully delivered to those who wanted their world to end at the city limits.

"Hi," Matt announced, entering with the saintly gusto of one who arises before dawn. "Thought I'd give Nikki her first swimming lesson today," he added as he reached for a mixing bowl, poured it full of cereal, doused it liberally with milk, and began crunching hungrily.

"Good idea," I muttered, emerged in the challenges of world and local crises. Each of the older children had taught the next child to swim with such expertise that they all had made the local swim teams, although the strokes were a bit unconventional.

"Wim, wim," yelled Nikki from her high chair, banging her spoon for emphasis.

Matt dressed Nikki in the latest-style suit that Laura had purchased with the last of her baby-sitting money. Since she always purchased everything with the last of her money, I had finally concluded that the first money had no value.

As I watched Matt struggle with the combination of Nikki and the one-piece suit, I decided to let someone else tell him that it was on backward, especially after he muttered to her, "If teaching you to swim is as hard as dressing you, I'll never make it."

But Nikki took to swimming as her rubber ducky took to the bath. She'd stand at the edge of the pool, announce, "Here go," and drop in, sputtering and kicking. Lisa said her stroke was more like a cat paddle than a dog paddle. Remembering the time we'd rescued the cat from the pool in the middle of the night, we laughingly agreed.

But Nikki was totally fearless and her "cat paddling" got her wherever she wanted to go. The twins would shout "Yea, yea" in encouragement, and Nikki would grin in triumph, yelling, "Yea, yea, here go," and we'd all laugh and cheer.

Finally, Nikki would emerge at the pool's edge, chilled and exhausted. I'd wrap her in her "California Baby" beach towel, and she'd snuggle against me in warm contentment while I dried her curls and brushed them into place. Then I'd recite nursery rhymes, and Nikki would stick her toes in the air so I'd grab them and do "Little Piggy" one more time.

· · ● · ·

In a family the size of ours, we never know when a new phase will hit, its duration, or whether the statistics on survival are available. We've been challenged by everything from Little League to adolescence, with liberal amounts of all the childhood tragedies and triumphs thrown in for good measure, with no Shakespearian critic available to predict into which category the current drama would fall.

Laura's Tennis Game became this season's attraction, with a plot containing certain dispensible elements. For instance, tennis could not be played without a racquet that cost $39.95, or without a coach who collected $6.00 an hour, or without white cut-off Levis.

"How ever does she do it?" I asked David as we watched Tracy Austin on TV annihilating an opponent twice her age.

"Practice, coaching, talent," shrugged David.

"No, I mean continue to win sans Levis," I commented cryptically.

"I don't think I'll comment on that," he grinned. "We might just find out. And you can be sure that that particular knowledge is expensive."

In the meantime, Laura practiced tennis six hours a day, coming home only to shower, sleep, and wash her Levis. She also bought Nikki some cut off Levis, a T-shirt that said "Tennis, Anyone?" and a plastic racquet and ball.

We began to attend tennis matches, and Lisa bought a racquet too. Lisa was definitely not of championship caliber, however, since she'd purchased her racquet at a garage sale, had terry cloth shorts, one ball, and no coach.

Nikki, dressed for the drama, would yell "Yea, yea" no matter who was playing. When Laura played Lisa, Nikki took care of any potential sibling rivalry by carrying off all the balls, yelling "Yea, yea, Nikki," as she disappeared beneath the bleachers.

While Laura and Lisa continued serving it out on the tennis court, the other three continued on the swim team. Matt, who had quite a reputation for broken bones and stitches in his younger years, quipped that diving gave him the unique opportunity to land on his head without simultaneously landing in the emergency room. Julie and Jill became the team's backstroke experts and were only partly responsible for the the team's last place finish.

But no matter what the outcome, Nikki was always there yelling "Yea, yea." Clad in her swimming suit and "California Baby" towel she would cheer for whomever was swimming and do her "cat paddle" at every interval in the race. She was invariably aided and abbetted in this departure from meet regulations by Julie and Jill.

• • ● • •

A picnic in the pines is the climax of every summer. Perhaps it is part of the California spirit—in order to prove California is the state that has everything it becomes prudent to check periodically on all the assets.

Nikki pointed to the fragrant pines, noting redundantly,

"Trees." She scampered off to chase squirrels and to collect pine cones. "Skirils run fast," she commented breathlessly.

"You can't catch squirrels, Nikki," instructed Julie.

"Julie catch skirils," Nikki pleaded.

Julie giggled. "I can't catch them either."

Nikki looked at her with mocking disdain.

"Here, Nikki, have a sandwich," I suggested.

"No, catch skirils," she protested.

David finally tore some bread into pieces and, as the squirrels came forward timidly, he picked up Nikki and crept toward them. "Nikki, squirrels are supposed to run free. See how happy they are playing in the woods? This is their home. We wouldn't want to take them away from a place where they are happy."

Nikki looked around at the towering pines. "Skirils happy," she announced with satisfaction.

Thus the summer passed as quickly as grains of sand slip through small fingers. Sometime that summer, Nikki became a toddler, leaving the baby behind forever.

. . • . .

Labor Day abruptly slammed the door on summer and gave warning that evenings hereafter would be touched by a threatening chill. The older children returned to school, and the house became sullen at their sudden desertion.

Nikki, too, could not comprehend what attraction could possibly be of greater importance than herself. She'd follow each child to the door, hope sketched on her face. As she heard another "Bye, Nikki" and collected another kiss, hope would fade and her lip would quiver and tears would collect in her eyes. Finally, when everyone had gone, she'd gather a stuffed toy and lay her head on the sofa, thumb in her mouth, looking desolate and deserted.

"Look what I have, Nikki," I'd say, holding up a book. She'd run to me, arms outstretched, and we'd read together from the same books the others had loved and rock in the same battered chair. Then we'd do finger plays and baby exercises and recite Nikki's favorite nursery rhymes.

As autumn beckoned, I got out the stroller. By now, of course, Nikki was too old to ride at the beginning of the journey, but coming home was a time to remember baby comforts. She would settle back sleepily, only occasionally pointing out sights she did not want me to miss.

This would remind me of the Great Aunts' last letter: "Ann, you must remember to stroll Nicole and identify objects for her. Not many mothers remember to stroll their children these days and enrich their environment." I thought about other "Great Auntism's" like "talking to babies makes them smart" and "read every day to even the smallest baby." I smiled as I remembered that the small, midwestern town outside of Chicago had honored Martha when she'd taught fifty years by celebrating Martha's Day.

Caroline, however, had quit teaching after forty nine years so that the town wouldn't have a Caroline's Day. But between the two of them they had taught other people's children for nearly one hundred years, living proof that giving birth to a child is not the only way to acquire the insights needed to raise one.

CHAPTER · 8

One morning as Nikki and I were preparing for our stroll, the phone rang. I answered, grasping a wiggling, impatient Nikki under my arm.

"Hi, it's Greg."

My heart thumped and I responded weakly, "Yes?"

"Nikki's court date has been set. I had nothing to do with it at all, but it's set for December 24."

I gasped. "That's Christmas Eve. How *could* they?"

"Well," he went on, "you *do* have the right to legal counsel. Foster parents can be represented in court by an attorney in this state."

"What about the agency? Don't *you* have an attorney?" I inquired.

"Yeah, but I think he's a law school reject. He's only won two of the ninety-four cases he's had, and I think those were by accident. His theory is always the same with every case. Get in there and get it over with. Winning never seems to be a possibility."

"Well, who *is* a good attorney? We've never even been to one and I certainly wouldn't consider any of the three David plays tennis with."

"I am not permitted by law to recommend an attorney. So let's call this a 'casual name dropping': Micah Madison," he muttered.

I scribbled the name quickly. "Should I thank you or not?" I asked.

"Let's hope we don't find out soon. There's still no word from Nikki's relatives, but that December 24 date has to be the work of the shyster they hired. We aren't home free yet. And that reminds me, make sure Micah—er, whoever—gets that date continued until after the holidays."

"Right," I answered with some hesitation. *Oh well,* I thought, *certainly a competent lawyer will know what continued means.* "I'll let you know what we're going to do after I've talked with David." As I hung up, I turned to Nikki. "Guess we won't be enriching your world today, Nikki. Have to try keeping you in it instead."

• • ● • •

As usual David's ever-efficient secretary put me through to him immediately, not knowing which child might have broken an arm. She once told me that that is the least she expects.

"David, Greg called and Nikki's court date is Christmas Eve and they may take her away because they have a crooked lawyer and the county lawyer is totally incompetent and so we have to get a lawyer who can get the date 'continued', so we don't have to go to court on Christmas."

"Are you sure you have the right number?" David can be so infuriating when he thinks I'm running on.

"David, please. This is serious!" I implored.

"Sounds like it's something all right," he replied. "Look, I'll come home for lunch. No, wait—" I knew he was mentally reviewing the contents of the refrigerator—"I'll *bring* something for lunch."

Over cheeseburgers and french fries, we decided that we did need a lawyer because we couldn't let Nikki go back to a place where she had been beaten and where she was so afraid of the people. David agreed to find out about Micah Madison. "What we need is a child's advocate, someone to make the right decision for Nikki," David muttered, chewing a french fry.

"And all along, I'd thought the agency would do that."

• • ● • •

As we drove to our maybe-lawyer's office, David explained that Micah Madison was the most highly thought of person for children's advocacy in the city. According to his secretary, Micah Madison wouldn't accept a case unless he believed in it. But David and I didn't even know if we had a case. And if we did, how would we convince this invincibly-portrayed stranger to help Nicole?

A briskly efficient secretary led us to his office, noting, "Mr. Madison will be back in a few minutes. He had to make a flying trip to the junior high to rescue one of his sons. Make yourselves at home."

I quickly assessed the office: two canvas-covered, yellow butterfly chairs; lawbooks, randomly collected in haphazard stacks throughout the room; and a desk burdened with more paper than I'd seen in ten years of teaching. On one wall was a large canvas obviously created by unlimited imagination and undisciplined talent, perhaps, I thought, the work of the young son he'd set out to rescue. On the other wall were fifteen—we counted them—pictures of boys in the cap and gown of one of our local high schools and two pictures of blond-haired girls, cheer-leader types, in the same garb.

"We thought *we* had a large family," I whispered to David.

"What are you whispering about?" asked David, looking around as if expecting to see someone.

"Seventeen kids." I pointed. "Maybe it's contagious." It seemed to me that our six were an ample number and I was not about to make any slightly suspicious comments by talking aloud and then finding eleven additional children on my doorstep when I reached home.

"Well," said David (inanely, I thought), "he probably likes kids."

Just then the door opened and a tall, rough-hewn man entered managing to convey a rather brisk piety as he extended his hand. "Micah Obediah Madison," he announced. "Sorry to keep you waiting."

"That's all right," I stammered. Then, while David

cringed, I went on. "We've been sitting here stunned by the pictures of your family."

Micah smiled broadly. "Most people tactfully ignore those pictures or comment about how handsome they are. No one has been honest enough to be stunned before. I'll probably take your case. " He explained, "My wife and I raised the two girls first and since then we've been collecting boys that are victims of the system. Some of those guys were runaways, some I bailed out of our local excuse for juvenile hall, some were beaten by parents, and some seemed destined for trouble unless someone collared them. Those on the wall are the ones who have made it at least part way out into the world. We have nine others at home right now." His eyes twinkled. "Including the one who just suggested in rather inappropriate language what he thought of the local school system. Of course, he's right; I just have to teach him to improve his vocabulary and his timing, however."

"How does your wife manage all those kids?" I asked incredulously.

"She has a Ph.D. in philosophy, teaches at the college, and mans the ivory tower guns at night," he commented dryly. "But let's hear about your little one—Nicole, I believe my secretary said."

So David told him the parts of the story that might be relevant to a lawyer, editing and disregarding those things that were meaningful only to us. He finished, "Well, one of the workers said we would need someone in court for Nikki's best interests and your name was mentioned . . ." His voice trailed off.

While David told our story, I observed Micah's reactions—appropriately placed grimaces, frowns, grins, and chuckles. Now as David finished, Micah slowly shook his head, stroking his chin thoughtfully.

Unable to endure the tension, I blurted, "Is that what you do when you decide not to take a case?"

"No, I'll take the case," he said finally. "And maybe we'll win."

"Maybe," protested David. "That isn't good enough."

"That's as good as you're going to hear in this charade of courts and judges and social workers and lawyers. Society heaps abuse on children at the same time it professes to rescue them. When a little child like your Nicole finds a home and people to call her own that's where she ought to stay. No one really knows anything about rehabilitating a natural parent; a few natural parents do it on their own ... not many, but some. I always try to see who the child is bonded to, where the child finds her identity—that's where the best interests of the child are. That's all I can do besides dig out relevant laws, argue with rhetoric-laced conviction, and hope we can get a judge who listens. That's usually the hardest part. We'll paper Dooley—that means make sure he won't hear the case; he's the worst judge of all. Problem is the rest aren't much better. But," he looked up, "I will get continuance on that courtdate. No one should have to endure this at Christmas."

As we left the office I asked David what he was thinking.

"I think we have the fight of our lives on our hands and an attorney equal to it," he answered solemnly.

"I can't seem to get beyond the *why*. Why should a little child—a baby really—have to be cast in a plot far beyond her years? Love is hers now."

I glanced at David, but he didn't respond.

· · ● · ·

Hearing a car pull up against the curb outside, I glanced up from the book I was reading to Nikki, carried her to the window, and watched the ample figure of Greg Adams emerge from the car and start up the walk.

I opened the door quickly to let Greg in, closing it behind him quickly to prevent the cold wind from sneaking in.

"Fall's here," he announced. "Thought I'd stop by and keep you up-to-date. Guess your lawyer told you he got the continuance until January 15."

"No, we haven't heard anything," I replied.

"That's Micah; you'll always be the last to know."

"Seems to me that *you* recommended him," I reminded him.

"I thought I was stammering into the phone and muttered someone's name incoherently," he grinned. "Micah's the closest person to a children's advocate we have around here. What we really need is a full-time children's advocacy program that someone like Micah would administer." He shook his head. "You know, there were two million cases of child abuse in the United States last year just like Nikki's. Or worse." He paused. "Ten thousand children, ten thousand," he repeated, " were killed. Now why don't we have a telethon to raise money to find the causes and cure of *that* kind of disease. Child abuse is just about as contagious as the measles. Or maybe it's even more contagious. One generation passes it down to the next and it almost becomes genetic."

"Greg," I interrupted, "what are Nikki's mother and grandmother really like? Certainly I've met them, well, at least I've seen them and I do know what Nikki's reaction is like."

He looked at me thoughtfully. "Nikki's mother is just a child herself—extremely immature and completely tyrannized by her mother. In fact, this is a classic case of the contagion of child abuse. Nikki's mother was abused by her mother, and she, in turn, abused Nicole. She has no idea who Nikki's father is and doesn't really want Nikki. In fact, she tried to give her up for adoption at birth, but grandma wouldn't permit it. The old lady wanted the money from welfare that Nicole would bring in."

"It sounds like you could almost have looked at the situation then and prevented it," I interjected.

"We aren't anywhere near prevention, except in social work classrooms where they work all kinds of miracles," he commented cynically. "Sometimes I think the only way is for the parent to change himself or herself. I've had cases like that. However, when the courts order people to go to mental health there isn't much chance for success. Oh, sometimes they do go, but it's just a matter of pretenses. The patient pretends mental health therapy helps; mental health pretends it has cured another patient. After all, mental health has to prove itself to get our tax dollars. Then the court pretends to believe the whole package, and the child is returned to the family. Great success story. And when we pick up the same child again in a few months, everyone has a chance to prove the whole thing over again. Only the child never gets to start over." He grinned. "Now you've got me on my soapbox."

"How do Nikki's mother and grandmother *live?* I mean, do they work?" I didn't really want to hear how unsuccessful rehabilitation could be.

"You've got to be kidding. They are tried-and-true members of the welfare generation. They live on Social Security that the grandmother gets because she's 'disabled.' She's always seemed all right to me, but some people can draw disability for some pretty unusual reasons. She doesn't get a fortune from Social Security, so that's why they want Nicole. Her mother can then get the $300 a month that comes with her," he finished.

"Well, why doesn't the agency protect the best interests of the child? I thought that the very term 'Child Protective Services' implied that." I was beginning to have some very serious reservations about the system.

"There are all kinds of things that get into the way: relatives, politics, social workers, the flunkies that run the agency, and even judges. There is no one in the system to say what is in the best interests of the child and have it count for very much. The child doesn't pay taxes or cast votes or even have much importance in our society," he finished.

"You don't *really* think that Nicole will be returned to them?" I asked fearfully.

"Not in January anyway, and hopefully, never. But don't let that lull you into thinking that it won't be a battle. Their lawyer is Harvey Rolich and he's able to turn around many of our "sure" cases. Like one I have now, where the mother has never even seen the kid. He was born when she was in prison and, when she did get out for about twenty days, she never went to see him. She got caught selling cocaine and is in the slammer again. Meanwhile the kid is almost three and has an attachment for his foster parents—what would you expect?—he's never known his real mother. So we go to court to free the child so he can have a home of his own. And old Harvey shows up talking about how the mother is reformed and pines away in prison for her long lost child and I wind up taking the kid to jail once a week to visit a parent he's never known. He screams all the time and the mother ignores him. And if I missed one week, Harvey would jerk us back to court so fast it would make your head snap. But I think Micah can manage him in January with that Lincoln-esque approach. By the way, have you thought about adopting Nicole?" He looked at me searchingly.

"Can we *do* that? I didn't even know it was possible. I've certainly seen enough of her mother and grandmother to know that they'll never be able to care for her properly." I sighed. "It's hard to say when and how it happens, but we love Nikki as if she *were* our own."

"Bonding to foster parents happens very quickly in the case of a young abused child," he explained. "And you're right—Nicole's relatives will never be able to care for her properly, but getting a judge to believe that is a whole other case." He sighed. "I suppose we'd better get through the January hearing before we start talking adoption." Glancing at his watch, he said, "I've got to be going, but I thought I'd get this court stuff out of the way before the holidays and then leave you in peace until January."

As I let him out the door, I thought, what if Nikki *could* be ours forever? What if she never again had to face the horrible unknowns that hurt and frightened her so much? What if there were adults who could help her gain happiness as a right? Or would happiness for Nicole be as fleeting as a butterfly conversing with a daisy—not a right at all, but merely a reprieve from the inevitable? I picked up Nicole and cuddled her, both for now and for some future time when I might not be there to do so.

CHAPTER · 9

We would always remember that Thanksgiving as the time the turkey disappeared. Like the rest of the family, it was dressed casually; whatever crumbs escaped peanut butter sandwiches usually ended up stuffing our turkey. At any rate, it was done. I took it out of the oven and set it on the counter.

"Honey, we've got time to make it to Morning Prayer," David called.

"Dressed like *this?*" I asked looking down at my jeans.

"Sure, God knows you in jeans," he shrugged. "The turkey will wait forty-five minutes." Little did we know.

Only Nikki was properly attired for the occasion, a dainty little Pilgrim in a long, yellow calico dress, matching sunbonnet, and crisp pique apron. She pirouetted in black patent slippers yelling "Shurch, Shurch," urging the rest of us to hurry.

After the service, we lingered to allow Nikki to fulfill her duties as unofficial greeter. Snug in the safety of Lisa's arms she offered a choice of kisses, hugs, or handshakes to all parishioners. Very few could resist the little Pilgrim in their midst.

Once home, I rushed to the kitchen to finish dinner. The turkey was gone! I peered into the oven; perhaps I'd put it back in unintentionally. But the oven, too, was empty. "David," I yelled, "the turkey ran away!"

"You're kidding." David looked around the kitchen as though he expected to be attacked by a turkey. "It *is* gone," he admitted, puzzled.

From the hallway, Lisa yelled, "The case of the missing turkey is solved!"

David and I dashed down the hall to find our two cats, Brutus and Cassius, completing a cat's gourmet dinner: the remains of our turkey.

We all just stared in dismay until Lisa quipped, "At least no one can say 'Cassius has a lean and hungry look.'"

We groaned when Matt added, "Dare I say, 'Et tu, Brutus'?"

That's when the water fight began, the rest of us against the Shakespearian defendants who had named the cats in the first place. Nikki stood in the line of fire, shrieking with delight.

When we finally sat down to dinner, David commented, "I feel slightly ridiculous giving thanks for hot dogs on Thanksgiving." But he bowed his head and we followed. "Thank you Heavenly Father for the gift of Nikki, for the joy and laughter and love she has brought us."

There was a chorus of "Amens" followed by "Please pass the mustard."

C H A P T E R · 10

Four Sundays before Christmas we herald the coming of the
Christ child by decorating the Advent wreath. David and I
were not yet married the year we searched all over San
Francisco for an Advent candelabrum, stopping at shop after
shop, searching every little nook and cranny. Finally, in a
dark, cramped shop we found it—copper-burnished, beckoning. "Oh, David, it's perfect for our first Christmas." I
smiled in victory.

"Break the price gently," David admonished the store's
bent, white-thatched owner.

The old man turned the candelabrum over, and we gasped
at the price—$35!

David and I looked at each other with dismay. It had
seemed so perfect, so meant-to-be.

"How much could you spend?" the shopkeeper asked
softly.

David emptied his pockets and I emptied my purse and we
began counting. "Exactly ten dollars and fifty-one cents—
no," he corrected himself, "ten dollars and one cent if we're
to get back across the bridge to Berkeley." Disappointed, we
turned to leave.

"Wait," the old man called. "I promised myself I'd never
sell the Advent candelabrum unless it was to be used to
journey to Bethlehem. You see, this one belonged to my
own family." His eyes misted. "My wife and children are
gone now, but, oh, those were fine times when we'd take out
the Advent candelabrum and decorate it, the best of
Christmas." He paused. "The price is $10.01, I believe."

As the years passed, the candelabrum acquired an even
richer copper luster as it proclaimed the beginning of each
Christmas season. This year, using remnants of Nikki's
calico dress, Laura and Lisa made an old-fashioned quilted
wreath. An angel dressed in yellow calico adorned the center

of a red velvet bow that was carefully stitched to the wreath. After placing the wreath gently over the candelabrum, they added the five Advent candles. One would be lighted each Sunday during Advent until four were glowing. Then on Christmas Day, the large candle in the middle would glow all day, proclaiming the end of the journey to Bethlehem.

The lighting of the first candle signified not only the reading of the Christmas story in Luke, but of our individual, more commercial journeys to share treasures from the stores for the rest of the family.

This year, at Laura's pragmatic urging, the children decided to draw names for gifts for each other. "Great!" agreed Lisa who had saved $2.90. "But *I* get Nikki."

"That's not fair," argued Matt. "*I* get Nikki."

"We're the youngest. We'll take Nikki together," the twins announced.

Laura, resisting all challenges to her administrative ability, announced firmly, "All right, *everyone* gets Nikki a gift and the rest of us will draw names." It was, as always, the perfect solution.

Later, as David was burrowed in the *Times,* I interrupted, "David, this is probably going to sound dumb."

"Probably," he muttered.

"David!"

Reluctantly he let the paper collapse.

"I want Nikki to get each child something special this year. I can't explain why, but I know it's important."

"Never argue with a woman's intuition," David sighed. "And I suppose Nikki will do this shopping alone?"

"No, of course not. We'll take her to The City." Everyone in California knows The City is San Francisco. Lesser towns have names and must be so identified. But there is just one City.

David moaned, as he always does when he visualizes currency evaporating from his wallet. But then he became suddenly thoughtful. "I wonder if we will always live on the edge of time with Nikki?"

• • • • •

The day of the trip to the City was silken with misty webs of fog, stretching from the sky and clinging to the highway.

Nikki, snug in her new "big girl" fuzzy coat, pointed out the window excitedly. "Froggy, froggy."

David and I laughed. All of the children had called foggy days "froggy" in their early years. It was oral family history, now with a new member to carry it on.

David parked near the Wharf, and I remembered a previous visit, when there had been just David and I. We'd wandered around most of the day, and when time finally decreed our departure, David had found the car without the slightest hesitation. What an incredible feat, I thought, to both park a car in the City and then find it too.

As Nikki clambered into her stroller, David looked at me for directions. "Where to?" he asked.

"Wherever." It was a standard question and response which had often led us into unpredictable circumstances.

That day we wandered aimlessly from shop to shop, waiting to discover Nikki's "perfect" gifts. Nikki's eyes were wide with wonder and bright with the reflections of twinkling lights and sparkling Christmas decorations. "Look, look," she would urge pointing excitedly.

"Pretty, pretty." Nikki smiled up at a display of silver-colored mobiles. I picked her up so she could see more closely.

I called to David. "Look! This mobile has little tennis players volleying on the end of wires. Wouldn't Laura like this?"

"Waura wike," Nikki affirmed decisively. David nodded and Nikki's shopping began.

The dress was red calico, rather than yellow, but the rag doll with dark curls was very nearly a miniature of Nikki on Thanksgiving Day. David held up the doll. Nikki's eyes gave silent approval, and a new member was added to Lisa's doll collection.

We helped Nikki choose the special edition of Tolkien that Matt had long craved. For the twins we found an album of the Nutcracker Suite, with two accompanying hand-carved Nutcracker soldiers to stand guard during ballet practice.

As David paid for Nikki's purchases, I freed her from the stroller and watched her dash for a brown bear with bright button eyes. With tremendous effort, she lifted the bear— much larger than herself—and darted toward the door. David turned just in time to apprehend the tiny shoplifter. "Well, we couldn't forget Nikki, could we?" he added as he paid for the bear as well. We stuffed both Nikki and the bear back into the stroller. For once, the twin stroller was convenient.

Out on the street we stopped to watch and listen to street artists, enjoyed a crabmeat cocktail, watched the ships unload their daily catch, and tied a silver balloon to the bear and Nikki. Finally, we sank gratefully onto the brightly hued plastic chairs of an outdoor cafe where David and I consumed huge bowls of clam chowder and Nikki ate her dinner and polished it off with a bottle. Then we went back to the car—without getting lost even briefly, because David, as usual, remembered where he had parked it.

· · ● · ·

Christmas and babies belong together; that's the way it has been since the beginning in Bethlehem. It is my belief that a home with a baby is doubly blessed at Christmas, first by the benediction of the Christ Child and secondly by the affirmation of blessing and promise manifested in the new child. As each treasure of the season unfolded, Nikki's delight caused the rest of us to feel as though we were enjoying each experience for the first time. Had we ever before had such a Christmas tree, filling the house with the fragrance of pine, standing so tall and proud? The fragile ornaments were nestled high on its branches while the more durable ones were placed in Nikki's reach so she could rearrange them to her heart's content. By the end of the season both tree and ornaments reflected the degree of intensity with which she had accepted this responsibility.

Nikki also loved the gaily-wrapped packages, and watching her unwrap empty boxes became a favorite pastime of the twins while I watched the season's supply of wrapping paper diminish rapidly. Some boxes were torn into with fervor; others were carried around until the paper became worn and dirty. Nikki seemed quite content opening empty boxes, a practice David claimed we should have begun years before.

A visit to Santa at a shopping center brought us both amusement and embarrassment. The long line to see Santa was alive with toddlers and infants—protruding from shopping carts or sleeping on fathers' shoulders—and a few giggling teenagers waiting to order new boyfriends for Christmas. As we took our place at the end of the line, Nikki's hand clung tightly to David's as she observed the chaos about her. Suddenly, she glimpsed Santa and, with quick realization, dropped David's hand and raced to the front of the line. Utterly uninhibited she reached up to Santa to be picked up. Bewildered by Nikki's sudden assault, he gingerly lifted her onto his lap where she firmly planted a kiss on his whiskered chin, slid down one red-clad leg, and dashed back to David. Other people in line laughed in good-natured merriment, but David and I, abashed and awkward, found the nearest exit. It was only on the way home that we began to laugh, first tentatively, and then so hysterically that David had to pull the car over to the curb and park because he could no longer both drive and laugh. Nikki eyed us speculatively and finally smiled in appreciation because apparently something quite amusing had happened to her parents.

· · ● · ·

The Great Aunts arrived two days before Christmas. (David and I guessed that last year's wait at the airline terminal may have had something to do with it.) Over coffee, the Aunts brought out favorite Christmas recipes. Caroline announced, "I thought we'd start baking this morning." She looked to Martha for confirmation.

Martha nodded. "About five dozen of everything, except the breads. A dozen loaves each of stollen, brioches, and cinnamon bread should be enough."

"Let me guess," David teased. "We're entertaining the entire state of California."

"Oh, David," Aunt Caroline sputtered, "people do drop in over the holidays and they expect a little treat."

"So we're giving them twelve loaves of bread?" he commented with mock exasperation.

Caroline turned to me for assistance. "I thought little trays of goodies would be nice. And David could even take some of them to the office," her voice caught for a second and trembled slightly.

"You'll have to excuse David," I apologized, eyeing him sternly. "He's just not used to Christmas baking. Make anything you wish and you'll discover that David consumes most of it."

David nodded, finally realizing that baking was an act of Christmas celebration for the Aunts as well as an affirmation of their indispensability.

Soon an assortment of aromas emerged from the kitchen and filled the house. Nikki could not be diverted from participating in the Aunts' adventure, so I finally buckled her firmly in her high chair where she could supervise and approve the project without sabotaging it.

I crept upstairs to wrap Nikki's gift to David and me—a photo-collage of Nikki trying on a hand-smocked dress; coloring Easter eggs; attacking her first birthday cake; "cat paddling" in the pool; redecorating her first Christmas tree. I smiled in remembrance as I studied each picture, reliving our year with Nikki, realizing one more time the special gift she was to our family.

My thoughts were still very much on the preceding year when David lit the Christmas candle on the Advent wreath that evening. As wick and flame united there was awe on the faces of the younger ones and remembrance on the faces of those who were older. All five candles now glowed softly, and for a moment each of us was lost in private contemplation. Then Matt's voice began the Lord's Prayer. As we concluded, cries of "Merry Christmas!" broke the serenity. To me this one moment on Christmas Eve had always symbolized Christmas: one brief time when idea and substance met, a time of both majesty and simplicity; a time to be clasped tightly, yet to be given away; a time to glimpse love and a time to share it.

· · ● · ·

The other moments of Christmas began about 5 A.M. when I awoke to Julie and Jill's excited whispers. "He's been here," they announced. I groaned and rolled over, determined to ignore the predawn chatter. Sometime later I woke again, this time to the smell of coffee and freshly-baked bread. I opened my eyes to see David standing by the bed, delicately balancing a tray of coffee and the Great Aunts' stollen. "Merry Christmas," he greeted and leaned over to kiss me, precariously tilting the tray. He recovered it momentarily only to dump its entire contents on my lap. Shrieking as the hot liquid penetrated the blankets, I jumped out of bed, shaking my head ruefully at the remains of "breakfast in bed."

Grinning I protested, "I would have gotten up. Honest. Next time, give me a chance before you throw breakfast at me."

"You'll never believe this wasn't intentional," David claimed, taking blankets and sheets off the bed as I searched for my robe. I had the feeling it would be a long time before I had breakfast in bed again.

In the living room downstairs, six children sat primly in chairs, Nikki firmly ensnared in Matt's arms. Only the Great Aunts sat comfortably, near the tree. It was the only time all year when the children became angelic images of the lively group I really preferred. At some time, they must have misread some nonverbal message and concluded that these few peaceful moments on Christmas Day would please David and me and perhaps even increase the value of their gifts.

"Anyone interested in presents?" David asked. The stillness evaporated as excited voices tried to guess the contents of the brightly-wrapped packages.

Nikki wandered from child to child collecting bits of paper, bows, and scraps of ribbons. "Let's open Nikki's gifts," I said as I led her to her growing stack of presents. Together we opened the first box and Nikki smiled gleefully as she pulled out a tyke bike. She quickly climbed on and just as quickly became a traffic menace to everyone as she swerved among wrappings and gifts and siblings and Great Aunts.

"Open the others, Nikki," Jill urged.

But Nikki ignored her and clung firmly to her new bike. Watching the others tear into mounds of packages, I realized that the ability to treasure each gift individually is lost early in life. Innocence gives way to sophistication and is soon gone forever. So we let Nikki enjoy the new bike and as the day passed we gradually opened her gifts, letting her appreciate each for itself and loving Nikki even more for the simplicity and the purity of her love.

CHAPTER · 11

After Christmas the Aunts announced that they were staying until the January hearing. "Those people are not going to take Nicole away while we have anything to say about it. And, believe me, I'm going to give the welfare people an ample piece of my mind," stormed Martha. "And remember, *I'm* the quiet one. Just wait until they get Caroline on that stand."

David and I exchanged bewildered glances.

Caroline took over. "We've taken every course on child abuse the university has offered this year. As a matter of record, we have twelve units each. And I want you to know that we both got all A's."

I wondered what Micah would think about these two unexpected witnesses. We would soon know because his secretary had called to inform us that he wanted to see us.

Neither Micah's office nor manner had changed. He rose, leaned over his littered desk, and shook hands, first with me and then with David. Privately I was pleased with the handshake because I'd always surmised that men who do not shake hands with women are inclined to be either chauvinistic or intimidated by them.

"They hired Harvey Rolich, huh?" Micah inquired and went on without awaiting an answer. "Harvey likes to make people cry. His clients have the saddest stories anyone has ever heard, that is after Harvey has embellished them. He even gets so he believes his own stories. Unfortunately, the judges also buy his fantasies all too frequently. He'll battle like a tiger for the right of the natural parent. In fact, he takes only two kinds of cases, ones for the natural parent and accident contingencies. Rumor has it that if any ambulance in town went into reverse it would crash into Harvey chasing it. Too bad it doesn't happen," he summarized cryptically. "You ever meet him?"

We shook our heads.

"Well, he's about 5 feet, two inches, a real clotheshorse, yet has a crew cut, probably the last crew cut this side of the 50s. I think he sees it as a symbol of the All-American, apple pie look.

He continued, "When someone like Harvey gets you on the stand, you have to be careful to answer only what he asks. Take your time and if you don't like the question, get him to reword it. Don't let him get control of you."

"I'm frightened," I admitted. "I've never even been in a courtroom before."

Micah appraised me carefully. "Being frightened is being smart; showing it is not. You'll be called child snatchers and anything else that rattles through Harvey's brain. The important thing is to try to appear calm. Harvey likes nothing quite as well as emotionally distraught adversaries. He'll have you two months out of some state hospital if you cry. On the other hand, if the natural mother cries it's agony over her lost child. Doesn't seem too fair, does it?"

"What's the weakest point of Nikki's case?" David asked.

"Whose case?"

"Nicole's, our little one," David replied, puzzled.

"This isn't even remotely Nicole's case. It's her family's case, the agency's case, and your case. Hey," he sipped his ever-present coffee, "this child doesn't want to go to court. If I'm to believe Greg's report, she's happy where she is. The family wants the child back because she's chattel, property, and besides she gets them three hundred dollars a month from welfare. You people have stolen their property and their income. The agency goes to court to perpetuate itself. The agency bends in the wind. Right now the wind is blowing for you. Don't count on it not shifting direction."

"I asked what you thought the weakest point of the case was," David asked persistently.

"First, there's that whole unfortunate set of circumstances where no real evidence of abuse was obtained in the first place, no pictures, no x-rays. Frankly, that DA must have had to hustle to get detention of the child at all. And then there's Sir Galahad Adams," Micah frowned. "He rode in on a white charger and broke up that visit. Harvey Rolich will pontificate about how his clients were denied access to the child."

"But Nicole was terrified of them," I protested.

"Ann, that will carry no weight, none. You both have to face the very hard truth that Nicole's best interests will only be served if we can badger the family, the agency, and the court into submission. The law states that reasonable visitation can only be discontinued if it is shown that the visitation is harmful to the child's best interests. We have to prove that visitation is detrimental and that's literally impossible when it's included in the plan of reunification. I think we can keep Nicole under care, but I can virtually assure you that we won't prevent visitation," he finished.

"I don't see why it isn't easy to prove that any contact with her family is detrimental to Nicole," David commented.

"That would be an admission on the part of the agency that they have failed to rehabilitate the natural family," Micah replied.

"Haven't they?" David protested.

"Of course, but they want to perpetuate the myth that they are making progress with the family. Then after two years the agency admits they have failed and the judge frees the child from the parent. Or returns the child anyway," he added. "It's a game and those are the rules. If we don't play by them, Nicole will be removed from you and the agency will find a foster family that accepts the rules. That's why it's too early to do anything about adoption."

I sighed, "I get weary thinking about it."

"You will, unfortunately, get a lot more weary living it," Micah replied sternly.

Somewhat reluctantly we told Micah about the Great Aunts. To our amazement, he laughed heartily. "I'll put them on the stand. At least they saw the child when she was bruised. Any testimony about their expertise in the field would certainly be construed to be prejudicial. But Harvey definitely deserves to meet the Great Aunts."

Micah stood up and stretched. "Have to pick my wife up at the college. One of the boys wrapped her car around a tree last night. Walked away with a chipped tooth," he said ruefully. "Then I'd like to stop by and visit Nicole for awhile. You know, I don't trust these welfare reports much. I like to see for myself."

"Sure, come on over," I agreed. David and I exchanged approving glances. Micah really *did care about our Nikki.*

Chasing a large red ball Micah had brought for Nikki, the two of them raced together in the front yard among the leaves no one had raked in the fall. As the chill in the air announced the end of afternoon, Micah strode to the door, Nikki slung over his shoulder. Micah warmed his hands by the fireplace while Nikki cuddled in my arms in the rocking chair and the Great Aunts prepared a snack of leftover Christmas goodies. Grabbing cookies and candies, the other children joined us and, inevitably, we began exchanging Nikki stories and soon hilarity warmed the room.

When Micah finally made his way to his battered van, dusk had given way to darkness. Clinging to each of Micah's arms was a Great Aunt on her way to the best Mexican restaurant north of La Paz, according to Micah.

Micah visited Nikki two more times before the hearing. One time they picnicked in the park on generous, but very untidy peanut butter and jelly sandwiches. Another time Micah and Nikki went shopping and bought a huge rag doll which Nikki christened "Waggy." Micah and Nikki were friends now, and Micah was a part of Nikki's life. The "best interests of the child" was no longer an abstraction. It had been translated into a red ball, laughter, peanut butter and jelly sandwiches, and rag dolls.

CHAPTER • 12

It rained the day of Nikki's hearing, California rain, cold and unrelenting. It was the kind of rain that could go on for a week and never falter in intensity.

The Great Aunts, hair immaculately coiffed by the best local stylist and dressed in Sunday best, had, since dawn been wearing out separate patches of the carpet by their intermittent pacing.

I had tossed and turned all night, sleep eluding me completely, while David snored beside me with maddening serenity. David picked up all his worries each evening and deposited them in the nearest wastebasket. He claimed he never had any difficulty accumulating new ones the next day. But I gathered all my worries at night and tucked them into my pillowcase, planning to solve them while I slept. But, unfortunately, my worries would creep out, one by one, and sneak into the corners of my brain, and I'd spend the night trying in vain to recapture them.

As I drank my sixth cup of coffee, I announced, "Other people go to court; we don't. I've never even been there and I don't want to go now."

"Just get in the car," David admonished. "If we don't go to court, what happens to Nikki?"

"What happens if we *do* go? We still might lose her," I protested.

"If you don't go we'll lose her for sure; if you do we could win her. No choice, Mom," Laura spoke with her usual assurance as she held Nikki close to her. "Anyway, I get a whole day off school to spend with Nikki." Smiling she added, "Why don't you wear shoes though, Mom? I've heard it impresses the judges."

I stared at my feet and, feeling slightly foolish, I dashed upstairs for some shoes.

I'd always thought courthouses were the result of a mad

architect's revenge on the county. Seeing the inside of one confirmed my suspicion. The elevators led to lonely corridors closed off by doors to private offices and restrooms. At infrequent intervals, there were unmarked doors that led us through the maze to a series of courtrooms.

David walked up and down outside the courtrooms reading papers pasted on the doors. He came back announcing, "We're in courtroom two."

"How did you find that out?" I asked.

"That's what those papers are for. They list what will happen in each courtroom that day."

"Who is the judge?" I asked.

"Anderson," David replied. "He isn't supposed to be the worst."

"That's a glowing recommendation," sputtered Caroline. "I couldn't get a job at the local five-and-dime with that."

"Well, don't let it bother you," replied Martha. "I'm sure the judge wouldn't have the qualifications for that either. Remember what we learned about the judiciary at the university."

"What?" I demanded.

"Not now, Ann, you are not old enough to know," Caroline announced firmly.

"Where is Micah?" My eyes scanned the halls.

"Probably in juvenile court making sure that everyone knows the case got bumped up to superior court because it is contested," Martha lectured.

David and I looked equally astounded.

"See," said Caroline in her best teaching tone, "if no one was trying to contest the hearing, since it's just an annual review, the juvenile court would hear it. But you people are saying that Nikki shouldn't be returned and her relatives are saying that she should. You don't agree so it starts in superior court. Understand?"

"Oh," was all I could manage. How had these two learned so much? I felt more than a little proud of the adventuresome duo.

"Here's the man," David said as Micah jogged toward us.

"Hi," he said breathlessly. "Want to bet this gets continued until this afternoon?"

"Why?" we asked in unison.

"Over there in the Budweiser cap, county bowling shirt, and tennis shoes is the county lawyer, Dennis Shirk. Anderson will never let him in looking like that."

We all stared.

"I wonder where he left his bowling ball?" Caroline asked.

"We may as well go in," Micah announced, holding the door open for us.

The courtroom did not meet any of my preconceptions. Its tall, arched ceilings were painted bus terminal beige. Large chandeliers had been converted ineptly into flourescent lighting, and row upon row of brown naugahyde chairs were leaking liberal amounts of cotton stuffing. The judge's bench looked as if it had been kicked by an angry child who left huge scuff marks.

An air of trepidation surrounded and engulfed me as nightmare and reality collided. How could Nikki's fate be decided in such surroundings? How could she be taken from us? What happened if law and love were in conflict.

My fears were interrupted by the bailiff's announcement.

"All stand, Superior Court, State of California, County of Apthorp now in session, Judge Dwight Anderson presiding."

We stood as the judge entered, bulbous nose leading, receding chin following, and a few strands of hair wilting on a near bald surface. He marched pompously to the bench.

There was a general groan and clatter from the ancient chairs as he motioned for us to be seated. I glanced around to observe Nicole's mother and grandmother. How young the girl was, not much older than Laura. No wonder she had wanted to give up Nicole for adoption. Her life should be carefree and happy. As though she felt my eyes on her, she turned to look at me, a faint smile fleeting across her face. For a moment I glimpsed Nicole in her eyes. Her mother elbowed her sharply. She looked away.

"Mr. Shirk, you are here as counsel for the county?" the judge asked.

"Yes, your honor." He removed his cap in deference to the judge.

"Are you compensated for your position?"

"Yes, sir, I am."

"Then I would suggest that you are demeaning your position as well as that of the court by your inappropriate attire. Court will be recessed until 1:30 so that Mr. Shirk can dress himself in a manner suitable for legal counsel. If you do not own such clothing and cannot afford it, I suggest that you enlist the aid of the Salvation Army in obtaining a suit." Judge Anderson sneered in contempt, his words rising with his temper, and strode back into his chambers.

Micah raced up the aisle, motioning for us to follow him. Caroline nodded to me. "Go ahead. Martha and I will stay here and stake out the situation." David and I attempted to catch up with Micah, running down the corridor in frantic pursuit, intercepting him just as the elevator door opened. Micah pushed the button, muttered something unintelligible, then turned to us.

"We'll probably get started this afternoon. I just don't like the unpredictable. It's like someone in a symphony missing a note. All may turn out well as long as he realizes his mistake, but what happens if he launches into a different symphony?"

"But you *do* think the case will be heard this afternoon?" asked David, anxious for a direct answer.

"Depends upon that county clown and his wardrobe. Shirk thinks he's making some kind of political statement dressing as he does. I expect Anderson will throw him off the case and the county will have to find a lawyer who owns a suit. See you at 1:15."

As Micah tore off toward juvenile hall, David commented, "Either bailing out one of his own or adding another."

Hand in hand, David and I walked slowly to the car, ignoring the rain as it poured down on us. Worry about

Micah's unfinished symphony and the effect of events beyond our control made us oblivious to all outside forces.

We drove home to spend a few minutes with Nikki, mentally measuring how many moments were left with her, hoping for a lifetime, hoping that love would win.

· · • · ·

Water splattered in waves against the car when we returned to court. The Great Aunts were waiting on a bench near the courthouse door. Martha leaned against the wall in exhaustion, and Caroline, holding her shoes neatly in her lap, stretched her legs and wiggled her toes.

Caroline spoke. "We had lunch with the nicest man. He's a retired school administrator and his hobby is coming over here to watch the "doings" as he calls it. Says Anderson likes to return kids to the natural parent."

"That's a dumb term, isn't it? At school last year we learned that 'birth parent' is a better one," Martha interrupted.

Caroline, annoyed, looked at her sharply. "Anyway, Marvin—that's his name—says there isn't much justice coming out of this building when it comes to children. Of course, that's a national trend, as Martha and I learned. There's not much justice for the child anywhere. Anyway, Marvin says the first time around, he'll probably leave the child in care. That's now. But later when it really counts, he's just like the rest of them, equates the family with patriotism and Americanism and refuses to be educated."

Martha, was anxious to deliver her share of gossip. "Says your lawyer cares about kids just about as much as anyone around but that he has a hard time getting those judges to listen to reason. Most of the judges physically discipline their own children and they have a struggle determining the difference between a swat on the bottom and submerging a hand in boiling water. Marvin says we ought to take Harvey Rolich back with us to Joliet for seven-to-ten for most every crime in the book and that "Shirk Jerk"—that's his nickname—ought to go to the nearest funny farm if he can pass the admission standards." She finished, "Oh, by the way, don't expect us for dinner. Marvin is taking us out for pizza."

Waiting for Caroline to don her shoes and attempting to digest this new profusion of information, I pressed the elevator button and we found our way back to the courtroom.

This time Micah was awaiting us. "Well, it looks as if Shirk got himself a black, double breasted, shantung suit and a scarlet satin tie from the Salvation Army. And I think he polished his tennis shoes, so we may be all set. Just depends on Anderson's mood. Oh, by the way, that handsome, sophomoric character over there is Nikki's attorney. He's the assistant DA, appointed by the courts to represent the child. He feels he does this best by never uttering a word at hearings. Come to think of it, it's really not so strange—his silence speaks for the child, who has no voice at all."

Micah left to find his place at the front of the room. Judge Anderson was already striding in. As he seated himself, he peered sternly at the county lawyer and hesitated. "Mr. Shirk, I am going to continue, but I will see you in my chambers immediately following the hearing this afternoon."

"Yes, your honor," Shirk replied meekly.

"The matter before the court is the annual review of Nicole Russell, Case No. 4917. Mr. Shirk, are all the parties ready?" the judge inquired.

The other attorneys nodded. "Yes, your honor," Shirk replied.

"Very well, Mr. Shirk, you may begin," Anderson ordered.

"I represent Child Protective Services and we are recommending that the juvenile, Nicole Russell, remain in foster care in her present home for another full year while the plan of reunification is implemented."

Micah stood. "Micah Obediah Madison. I represent the foster parents, David and Ann Johnston, and we concur with the position of the county, although we have some grave reservations about visitation procedures."

The short, graying man with a fresh crew cut, outfitted in an impeccably hand-tailored suit spoke. "Your Honor, I am Harvey Rolich and I represent Helen and Marilyn Russell, the dear mother and grandmother of this child. They have been robbed cruelly of her love for more than a year and have even been deprived of visitation. And on what grounds? The child fell from her crib and the grandmother, with that wonderful spirit of grandmothers everywhere, caught her, causing a few bruises. Should she have let the child fall and shatter her tiny bones? What we see here is a woman punished for an act of courage. And what about the young mother here who cries for her child daily? I ask that you make a decision here and now to return this child to the loving environment from which she never should have been taken."

As he concluded, David nudged my arm with a note from Caroline: "Seven-to-ten in Joliet is not long enough." I tried to smile at her, but I had no smiles left.

"Objection." Micah rose at the same moment the gavel fell.

"We are not now going to decide the hearing, Mr. Rolich," Anderson admonished.

Anderson turned to the assistant DA. "Mr. Wallace, I assume you agree with the county's position?"

Mr. Wallace nodded and left the courtroom. And that was Nicole's representative, I thought.

"Mr. Shirk, you may call your first witness."

"I call Mr. Gregory Adams."

Greg went forward calmly, and took the oath, and proceeded to the witness stand.

As Greg recounted the events of the year, I relived that first night when Nikki came to us bruised, beaten, and despairing of life. How could anyone believe the story that the grandmother and daughter were trying to sell? As Greg droned on and on in answer to Shirk's questions, I wanted to cry out, "None of us should be here. Nikki needs me at home. She's happy. We're happy. Don't get in the way. *Understand.* I love her so much my throat aches from stifling sobs of fear that someone can take her away. Just stop this so the pain will leave." But my silent plea went unheeded.

When Shirk finished the questioning, he turned to Micah who muttered, "No questions."

Mr. Rolich stood, pulled down his jacket sleeves with an exacting gesture, and attacked. "Tell me, Mr. Adams, how does it feel to be a child snatcher?"

Greg replied, "We were acting in the best interests of the child when we removed her from her home."

"Mr. Adams, how many other children have you stolen— literally ripped from their mother's arms—this year?"

Greg looked to Shirk for assistance, but he was busily shuffling papers.

Micah, casting an incredulous look at Shirk, interrupted. "I object to this line of questioning as being irrelevant to the case and insulting to the witness."

"Sustained," Anderson agreed. "Keep your questions relevant to this case, Mr. Rolich."

"I'll try, your honor, but my heart aches for this mother and for every mother who has her child snatched by the state." Rolich took his handkerchief from his pocket, removed his glasses, dried his eyes, and went on, his voice quivering melodramatically.

As the afternoon proceeded, Rolich's theatrics accelerated in intensity and Greg sat on the stand unflinching both in his story and in his handling of the case.

"Is it true, Mr. Adams, that you once took this child from her dear mother's arms in the middle of a visit and returned her to the foster mother?"

"Yes, but . . ."

Mr. Rolich turned to the judge in triumph. "You see, he admits it. The dear mother was so upset at such a cruel turn of events that she was emotionally unable to visit her child again. She could no longer endure your cruelty. First you took her child and then you took away her right to visit that child. No more questions," he announced with a grand flourish.

"Are there any other questions for this witness?" Judge Anderson peered at the three attorneys. Micah glared at Dennis Shirk, who shook his head.

Micah turned to the judge. "I have some questions, your honor."

"That's why Micah didn't ask questions before," Caroline whispered. "He'd figured that Shirk wouldn't attempt to rebut Rolich."

Micah rose from his chair with deliberation. "Mr. Adams, I'd like to go over a few points. I have here an affidavit from the emergency room doctor, a Dr. John Winslow. Please explain under what circumstances it was obtained?"

"It was obtained December 24, 1978, when I took Nicole Russell to the emergency room accompanied by Officer Larry Franklin of the sheriff's office, whose statement you also have," Greg replied.

"Objection, your honor." Rolich was on his feet immediately. "This alleged affidavit has already been submitted in evidence by the county. There is no reason to take the court's valuable time to review what has already been submitted as presumed evidence or manufactured evidence."

"Your Honor, I am only asking for clarification of the evidence in the affidavit," Micah responded.

"Objection overruled. Proceed, Mr. Madison," the judge ordered.

"The emergency room doctor states that, in his opinion, there is no way the injuries to the child could have been caused by accidental means. Was that the opinion he stated the night of December 24, 1978?"

"Yes, sir, it was," Greg replied.

"Objection." Mr. Rolich was on his feet again. "Mr.

Adam's testimony is hearsay. Again I'd like to point out that Madison is beating a dead horse. The county has already submitted that questionable affidavit into evidence."

"Sustained," Judge Anderson ruled.

Caroline turned to me, again whispering, "That's all right. Micah got what he wanted; a statement that Nikki's injuries were not accidental."

"Now tell me about the visit on March 6," Micah directed.

"During that visit the child's clothes were removed by the relatives and, as a result, she got pneumonia," Greg began.

"Objection, your honor. Mr. Adams did not even supervise that visit," Rolich stretched to his full five-feet, two inches of indignation.

"Sustained," came the ruling.

I looked at David incredulously.

But Micah appeared totally unruffled. "Did you supervise the visit on March 20?"

Greg replied, "Yes, I did."

"What happened at that time?" Micah asked.

"Nicole became so hysterical that I was unable to leave her with her grandmother and mother. At that point it would have been detrimental to the child to proceed with the visit."

"No more questions, your honor." Micah spoke quickly as Rolich was on his feet again. Rolich glared at him, but did not speak. Both lawyers sat down, and Greg returned to a seat directly in front of us.

"Does the county have any other witnesses?" the judge inquired.

"No, your honor," Mr. Shirk replied.

Greg buried his head in the seat in front of him, then turned to us looking exhausted and defeated. "Ann, you'll probably be on the stand the rest of the afternoon corroborating my story. Shirk can't even win a sure thing."

"I can't go up there," I protested.

"Yes, you can," Caroline asserted firmly. "For Nicole," she added.

"Do you have any witnesses, Mr. Madison?" Anderson asked.

Micah stood, and I cringed as he said, "I call the foster mother, Ann Johnston."

Every muscle trembled as I walked down the aisle to take the oath. I felt as though I might dissolve into a writhing mass at any moment. I was walking into a forest of fear and I felt it engulf me. As I raised my hand to take the oath, my hands and knees shook uncontrollably; walking to the witness box, I entered my own Auschwitz.

"State your name," I was commanded.

Then Micah began, question by question, to go over the events of the year. Soon I forgot where I was. Once again it was Christmas Eve and Nikki's screams of terror, her fear of food, the terrible bruises, her pneumonia, the emergency room, more and more terror-laden moments became my reality. Somehow, a voice that I couldn't believe was mine was speaking quietly and with self-assurance.

Finally, it was over. Micah had finished.

The judge asked, "Are there any other questions for this witness?"

Shirk, predictably, shook his head.

Rolich rose menacingly. "I have questions, your honor," He glared at me. But fear had left me and, at least for that moment, it could not return. It was my child, *my* child, who was in danger, and I was the only one who could do anything about it.

Rolich dug in. "How do you know that the alleged bruises were inflicted by the grandmother or mother? Have none of your own children ever been bruised?"

"Yes, of course they have. But at six months Nicole did not have the mobility to fall. She couldn't even turn over," I replied firmly.

"Mrs. Johnston," he went on, "isn't it true that you don't want the mother and grandmother to visit their child?"

"We have cooperated with the agency in every visit that

was scheduled, but I want Nicole well taken care of and they don't seem to know how to do it."

"You mean they don't do it your way," Rolich summarized triumphantly.

"Visits disturb Nicole so badly that she is hysterical for days afterward. As I testified before, I believe they are extremely detrimental to her. It's not a matter of my way or their way. It is what is right for the child."

Rolich shook his head in deep pity at such an absurd observation and sat down.

"No more questions?" the judge inquired. "Then the witness is dismissed."

I stepped down from the box into clouds of exhaustion and only dimly I heard that it was 4:30 and that the hearing would be continued at 8:30 the following day.

We were in the elevator, Great Aunts included, before Micah spoke. "I'm going to subpoena Ben Lyons for tomorrow. We're going to have to try for some hard proof of Nicole's reactions and abuses." He turned to me. "You did a good job of standing up to Rolich. I think, if we win, your testimony will have turned the tide."

As the elevator door opened, Micah scurried away and David herded the rest of us into the car. "For those who don't have pizza invitations, it's take-out Chinese," he announced, knowing it was my favorite. How could I tell him that overwhelming fatigue *had* no favorites?

CHAPTER · 13

The rain fell steadily, lashing at the windows. As I listened to its ceaseless pelting, I hoped it would awaken Nikki so I could comfort her. Instead the rain lulled her into a deep, peaceful sleep. Beside me David too slept, seemingly without concern.

"Hey, God, are *you* awake?" I raised up on one elbow. Some theology that reflects, I cautioned myself. But I was feeling so very alone. For some reason I'd been remembering a sentence from the writings of Paul Tillich: "The law of love is the ultimate law because it is the negation of law; it is absolute because it concerns everything concrete."[1] I certainly was willing to surrender to the "ultimate law," but what about Anderson? Which law would *he* choose? Did he care about love? Did he care at all about Nikki? "Hey God," my brain called, "are you awake? Near God or Far God, where *are* you?"

Morning came and the rain was still falling with unrelenting ferocity. As we prepared for court, I drank several cups of coffee, trying to wash the webs of fatigue from my brain. Only Nikki remained totally unconcerned, totally unaware, totally cheerful. Even the Great Aunts were victims of battle fatigue.

At the courthouse, Micah was pacing impatiently in the corridor. "Thought you were going to leave me to do a three-hour monologue," he frowned.

"Did you subpoena Ben Lyons?" I asked.

"Yes, he'll be here when we need him. It's an on-call subpoena, so he doesn't have to show up until it's time to appear."

He turned to David. "You're up first. It won't be long, though, because I've already covered everything with Ann.

---

[1]Tillich, Paul, *Systematic Theology. Vol. I* (Chicago: The University of Chicago Press, 1951), p. 152.

Just be sure to answer my questions thoroughly. Ann projected enough credibility for our case that Harvey may not want to risk a cross-examination with you."

We were interrupted as Dennis Shirk approached in an obviously new, brown tweed suit and brown loafers. "Wow, Anderson laid one on me yesterday. Said to get a decent suit or he'd have me suspended. Talk about being petty. Oh well, I kind of like it, and they do say that clothes make the man." Micah stared without comment. After an awkward moment, Shirk shrugged and walked away.

"We should be so lucky," Micah finally commented, "that anything as simple as clothes would make Dennis Shirk anything more than he already is. It's what's inside that counts, and so far Dennis doesn't seem to have much going for him. Well, let's get in there before Rolich decides the case himself."

Gloom sat in every corner of the courtroom sending out messages of depression and despair across the room. One shabby flourescent light blinked on and off indecisively. Dampness crept about the room on tiptoe, attacking unsuspecting victims with chills and shivers.

The bailiff entered with full ceremony, followed by Judge Anderson who looked about warily, his eyes finally resting on Dennis Shirk. Satisfied, he proceeded to the bench. "We are continuing the case of Nicole Russell. I'd like to remind counsel that this court has a full schedule and to limit arguments to the case before us and to avoid yesterday's theatrics. Are you listening, Mr. Rolich?"

"Sir, I always listen," replied Rolich.

"Mr. Madison, do you have other witnesses?" the judge inquired.

"Yes, I call the foster father, David Johnston."

David went forward, almost jauntily, and Micah asked him about the night Nikki had arrived and about her fear and terror after the visits and about the pneumonia. David answered fully, completely in control. Sleeping at night, I thought, did have something to commend it, like sounding sensible the next day.

Neither Shirk nor Rolich had further questions so David was home free. Micah explained later that the primary caretaker, and that was me, always carries the burden in cases like Nicole's. But I'd already figured that out myself.

Caroline and Martha drew straws to see which of them would testify. Micah thought having them both testify might make Anderson even more irritable and disinclined to listen. Caroline won. She also cheated, but I decided not to reveal that.

Caroline proceeded to the stand as though expecting coronation. She took the oath with dramatic solemnity and proceeded to the witness stand where she sat down majestically.

Micah began with the night that both Nikki and the Great Aunts arrived, and Caroline described in minute detail each of Nikki's bruises.

Rolich was again on his feet. "I object, your honor. We've already conceded that the bruises happened during the grandmother's courageous act to save the child from serious injury."

Before the judge could reply, Caroline spoke sharply to Judge Anderson. "Can't you control this man and his flagrant theatrics? Why, I wouldn't have put up with him in my classroom for ten minutes. Perhaps you need a course in courtroom control," she suggested, her voice tinged with sarcasm.

Anderson banged the gavel, the full impact of the blow striking his other hand full force. Ashen with pain, he shouted, "No more theatrics and no more unsolicited comments from the witness or I'll hold you all in contempt—including you, Shirk." Shirk looked around, totally baffled.

Micah wasted no time. "Miss Emory, this past year you did some intensive university study in the area of child abuse. Of particular focus was the matter of bonding. Would you please share with the court what bonding is, what it involves?"

"Objection. Do a few college classes make the witness an expert in the field?" Rolich demanded. "Besides she is hardly an unprejudiced witness."

"Sustained." Judge Anderson was concentrating on his bruised fingers which he had submerged in his drinking water. "Get on with it, Mr. Madison. None of this bonding junk. Everytime you come into my courtroom, you try to sneak it in. No more." Anderson's tone was threatening.

Micah looked defeated. "No more questions," he conceded.

Rolich rose. "Since I can't understand what this witness was doing here in the first place, I have no questions."

"The witness is dismissed." When Caroline stepped down she took a detour toward the attorneys' table where she seemed to stumble. As all the attorneys quickly rose to assist her, Martha and I saw her plant the heel of her shoe firmly into Harvey Rolich's instep, Caroline responded to his grimace with a satisfied, cat-like grin.

Just as Micah called his name, Ben Lyons, the last witness for the defense, entered the courtroom and was sworn in.

Micah began questioning him. "Could the bruises you saw on Nicole Russell on December 28 have been sustained in a fall from her crib?"

Judge Anderson sat up alertly.

"The child had the development of a newborn. There is no way she could have fallen out of the crib. Also, the very nature of the bruises would indicate that they were not the result of a fall," he explained. "In addition, the child weighed nine pounds after a birth weight in excess of seven. She was obviously undernourished."

"What would a child who had a birth weight of seven pounds normally weigh at six months?" Micah inquired.

"I'd have to wonder at much under fourteen pounds," he replied. "And most weigh more."

Rolich still did not move.

"Tell me about the night of March 6," Micah commanded.

Ben told of our call, of Nicole's pneumonia and her hysteria. He concluded, "When I first saw this child in December, I thought she was acutely retarded, but I've watched her grow into a happy, bright little girl."

Rolich rose. "Dr. Lyons, how long have you been a pediatrician for the Johnston family?"

Ben looked at me. "How old is Laura?"

"Just seventeen," I answered.

"Sorry," Ben grinned. "Kids grow up so fast." Addressing Rolich, he answered the question. "I've been their pediatrician for seventeen years."

"Are you personal friends?" Rolich persisted.

"No," replied Ben firmly.

"You've known these people for seventeen years and you don't consider them to be friends?" Rolich asked with calculated sarcasm.

"Well, not socially. But, of course, they are friends," Dr. Lyons admitted.

Rolich rose. "I move that this testimony be stricken from the record. This is not an unbiased medical opinion, but the opinion of a friend."

"Overruled," Anderson announced. "I've taken all my kids to Ben Lyons and have yet to share a cocktail with him. If you have no more questions for Dr. Lyons, please call your first witness."

"Yes, your honor, I call the baby's dear grandmother, Helen Russell."

The grandmother waddled forward, took the oath, and planted herself in the witness chair.

"Now tell me about December 24, 1978," Rolich began. "What really happened, Mrs. Russell?"

"I caught my beloved granddaughter as she fell from her crib." Her sob became a wail that permeated the courtroom.

The grandmother wailed and sobbed intermittently until Rolich went forward to pat her pudgy hand.

He turned toward Anderson. "No more questions for this poor, bereaved woman."

Micah shook his head as Anderson's eyes met his. "No questions."

Shirk rose. "I have questions, your honor."

Greg Adams gave a low moan and turned to whisper to us. "Even an idiot knows you don't question a sobbing old woman. I don't know what that qualifies Shirk for."

But Shirk was raring to go. "How often did you beat this child?"

Rolich yelled, "Objection!"

"Sustained," Anderson ruled. "Please reword your question, Mr. Shirk."

"Did you ever try to kill the child?" Shirk persisted.

"Objection."

"Sustained."

Undaunted Shirk went on, "Have you beaten other children?"

"Objection."

"Sustained."

"No more questions, your honor," Shirk turned to Adams, gave him the victory sign, and sat down in triumph. Greg shuddered.

"Do you have any other witnesses?" Anderson asked Rolich as the grandmother, appearing dazed, left the stand.

"Yes, I want to call the mother of the child." He turned and held out his hand. "Come on up here, little Marilyn."

Marilyn walked forward, head down, a waiflike figure, a child. She mumbled the oath and looked around bewildered from the witness box.

"Now, Marilyn, this must be hard for you," Rolich began oozing sympathy.

"Is this where I'm supposed to say that I want Nicole back?" she asked, fear looming in her eyes.

Although visibly embarrassed, Rolich recouped quickly. "Little Marilyn, I know that's what you want to testify to. But you just wait for my questions."

"Just like the ones we practiced in your office?" she asked.

"Well, now, your honor, you see this little girl was so frightened that I had to give her examples of the kind of questions that my child-snatching colleagues here could ask her," Rolich mumbled in explanation.

I reached out for David's hand. "She's just a child too, David," I whispered. "And look how she's being manipulated."

Anderson pounded the gavel. "Rolich, just get on with your questions!"

"Marilyn, I want you to tell me why you did not visit your child after March of last year," Rolich inquired.

"I was scared of him," she answered pointing to Greg. "Both my Mom and me were scared to death of that man. He came in when we were visiting Nicole and took her right away from us one time."

"So you were deprived of your child for a whole year because of Mr. Adams," Rolich summarized.

"Yes, sir."

"That's all, your honor," Rolich concluded.

"Any other questions for this witness?" asked the judge. Shirk shook his head; Micah rose.

"Tell me about the kind of baby Nicole was. Was she difficult or easy to care for?"

"Really difficult," replied Marilyn.

"Tell us about it," Micah encouraged.

"She screamed all the time. And it wasn't easy and . . ."

"Objection, your honor. Mr. Madison is leading my witness."

"Objection overruled," stormed Judge Anderson.

Micah went on and on and suddenly I wanted him to stop,

but there was no way to halt the pain for any of us. At Micah's urging, Marilyn testified to her need for the three hundred dollars that she would receive for Nicole each month. Why couldn't society help a young girl already caught in the welfare cycle without involving a baby she didn't really want, a baby *we* loved dearly. It seemed so impossible and so incredible that there were no solutions.

Rolich protested again. This time Anderson himself had had enough. "Sustained," he ruled. "We've heard enough, Mr. Madison. If there are no further witnesses, please keep the final summations brief." He sighed. "Mr. Shirk."

Shirk stood. "The county requests that the child remain in foster care for another year in her present foster home with the current plan of reunification with visitation and mental health treatment to be arranged," Shirk exploded in one breathless statement.

"Mr. Madison."

"We have seen evidence that this child was both abused and neglected and that visits continue to be detrimental to her. There are serious legal questions relevant to the visit of March 20. If Mr. Adams had not terminated that visit, could he not have been guilty of contributing to child abuse? I submit that Mr. Adams had no recourse. He had to make the decision that day, that moment, and he made it in the best interests of the child.

"My recommendation is that the child, Nicole Russell, remain in care another full year in the Johnston home. I have personally observed her at that home on three occasions. The child loves this family and is loved in return.

"Visits by the relatives have proved to be detrimental to her and should be discontinued or held in a manner that will protect the child against psychological or physical abuse.

"A welfare check should never be the motive to return a child to birth parents. Yet we have heard this young mother tell us that she needs the three hundred dollars from welfare, money that she would receive if Nicole were returned to her. But I ask the Court if it has found any evidence that she is ready to become a mother? I submit that there has been none. It is in the best interests of the juvenile, Nicole Russell, that she remain at the Johnston home where she is loved for herself. That's my full recommendation, your honor," Micah concluded.

Rolich rose solemnly, head bowed as though in prayer. Finally he looked up, trembling slightly as though guided by divine inspiration.

"This case is one of the worst travesties in juvenile history, your honor. We have no real proof of any neglect or abuse. Nicole Russell belongs at home with her loving mother and her loving grandmother. Marilyn Russell is terrified of Mr. Adams. She cannot even visit her child. Here we have totalitarianism at its worst, the state reaching out its tentacles, grabbing an innocent child, and depriving her of that special love that only a mother can give, a *natural* mother.

"I ask that Nicole Russell be returned to the home she never should have been taken from and that it be ordered accomplished in thirty minutes from this time," he finished dramatically.

Moments passed. The judge, seemingly deep in concentration, stared over our heads at some fixed point in space. Finally, he spoke. "The child, Nicole Russell, will remain in care until one year from this date when the case will be reviewed again according to the two-year plan of rehabilitation set forth by Mr. Adams. In view of the child's attachment to her foster parents, I recommend that she remain with them. However, I am deeply disturbed that so little has been accomplished in terms of rehabilitation. In the order I ask the continuation of the original plan of reconciliation set forth by Mr. Adams. I am also requesting that Child Protective Services remove the present worker from the case since it has been proved to my satisfaction that the natural mother, Marilyn Russell, fears Mr. Adams. Case dismissed."

As he and his entourage of bailiff and clerk left the courtroom, the rest of us sat stunned. Greg left first, tears streaming down his face.

Harvey Rolich left the room, his clients clinging to either arm, each clutching a sodden box of tissues.

Micah motioned for us to leave. "One step at a time," he encouraged. "We won this one. Go home to Nicole and love her."

And that's what we did.

CHAPTER · 14

Simultaneously introducing herself and proceeding into the house, the new worker announced, "I'm Toni Telford." She wandered aimlessly around the room picking up and examining each knick-knack with the expertise of a greedy auctioneer. Finally she settled gracefully in a chair, carefully soothing the skirt of her elegantly tailored suede dress. She scrutinized each fingernail assiduously and, satisfied with perfection, bent to remove a piece of lint from her shoe, frowning slightly at a barely noticeable wrinkle in her hose. I felt slightly uncomfortable in my jeans, David's old USC sweatshirt, and hair that cried out for a trip to the beauty shop.

Finally she proceeded. "Greg gets too emotionally involved in his cases. My position will be that of impartial observer and mediator. I have already visited Nicole's home and found it to be adequate. I always feel a child's own home is the place for her. So the visit will be there next Tuesday from ten until two."

"And are you going to supervise that visit?" I couldn't believe the woman's decision.

"Well, I'll be picking the child up at your home and returning her. And, of course, I'll stay for a while to see how everything goes," she replied in a no-nonsense tone.

"But," I protested, "Greg told me that the grandmother and mother lived in a shack. He said that when he was there the place reeked of alcohol and was littered and filthy. He told me that Nicole couldn't visit there, that he'd told the grandmother she'd have to find a better place and keep it clean."

"That's just Greg's opinion. I've formed my own. It was a violation of confidentiality for him even to discuss it with you. I consider the matter closed," she asserted.

"But what about Greg's report on Nicole's reactions to visits?" I persisted.

She yawned. "Greg's reports are always exaggerated. I feel that a child always is better off in a home that is really his, a *birth* home. Foster care has nothing to recommend it."

"But what about the things that have happened to Nikki? After all, Nikki's abuse is a fact. And I was there the day they undressed her in the middle of winter and she got pneumonia. And, believe me, I was there during the ensuing pneumonia, every weary moment of it," I protested.

Then she began to crumble a bit. "What do you really know about foster care, Mrs. Johnston? Let me tell you what it's like to grow up in a foster home. No one wants you for yourself. You learn to play the game, to be the sweet young girl, the pride of the system, and that gets you a stipend to go to college. And," her voice became even more sarcastic, "that stipend requires you to come back and work for the agency to repay it. And as long as you don't break the rules, they keep promoting you. Every day of your life is controlled; all your decisions are made for you. You can never step over the line and be a human being."

"I don't think all foster experience is like yours was, Ms. Telford," I defended. "I don't think there is a child in the world who has received as much love as Nicole has; we love her as much as any of our birth children, sometimes, I think, more."

"But don't you see, you have no right to love her at all; she isn't yours," she reminded me.

And I knew our conflicts were too deep, our differences too great, and that Nikki was not going to come first.

"I'd like to see the child now if you don't mind," she said from behind the barrier between us.

"She's napping right now, but I'll awaken her," I agreed. "Please do."

I returned with Nikki clinging sleepily to Big Bear. She

104

cuddled on my lap, sucking her thumb and staring warily at the stranger.

"She's a very dependent child, isn't she?" Ms. Telford observed.

"No, as a matter of fact, she's very independent. Most children act like this when their naps are disturbed."

"Come to me, Nicole," the social worker commanded.

In reply, Nikki buried her head in my shoulder.

"Hmm. Just as I thought. Please have her ready when I arrive on Tuesday," she said as she prepared to leave. "I can't afford to waste any time."

I let her find her own way to the door.

That evening David listened carefully with increasing annoyance. "Why didn't you call Micah?" he berated.

"I guess I just didn't know what to say."

"Well, *I'll* call him right now." David marched to the phone fuming with anger.

"Sure, thanks," I heard him say. He returned, "His wife said he's out playing Batter's Up with some of the boys. He left orders not to be disturbed while he was hitting home runs. She says that shouldn't be long."

The phone rang in just a few minutes. "Guess Micah struck out," I quipped as I answered. I recounted the day's events, and Micah listened without comment until I finished.

"So they gave you Tilly the Hun—that's Toni Telford's well-earned nickname. Do you remember the Garcia case, where the neighbors actually tape recorded a mother beating her child to death? That was Tilly's case. She refused to listen to anyone." Micah's voice was distant.

"Yes, I remember. Who could ever forget?" That case had made a headline in every newspaper in California. And the horror of the tape played on television was enough to convince even the most confirmed skeptic that child abuse is a terrible problem.

Micah continued. "There's a case now that I'm fighting where Tilly wants to return a schizophrenic child to a schizophrenic mother. There's not a hope in creation that the mother will ever care for that child and, what's even worse, Tilly knows that. Oh, I could go on. She's made the statement that she hates all foster children. She was one herself. Tilly thinks there is nothing worse than a foster home. It's sad, really," he paused. "When you begin talking about abuse, it never stops, and if I were a philosopher I'd say even unto the seventh generation." He sighed a long, weary sigh. "As for the visit, there's not a thing we can do about it except hope that Nikki comes back with a broken arm."

"Are you kidding?" I asked incredulously.

"We need hard evidence. That would be one way to get it," he replied. "And a lot better than most other ways. Kids get over broken arms."

Fear and hopelessness gripped me as I hung up the phone. What kind of society needed a little abuse to prevent greater abuse? And how could someone like Toni Telford be in a decision-making position? I tried to imagine Toni as a young child, a Nicole, left to fend for herself in an impersonal welfare system. Eventually she had learned to protect herself by conforming to the demands placed upon her. She learned to do whatever was required of her. And that was how she now approached her job—she would do whatever it required, no matter what the cost. The wraithlike child who was once Toni Telford had disappeared. The system had changed her beyond recognition. It had taught her to survive, but it had taken her heart.

· · ● · ·

The March wind was playing with budding branches in whimsical frolic the following Tuesday when Nicole and I went outdoors to await Toni Telford. The dreaded day had arrived. Nikki was going to a place I'd been told was unfit for a child, to people she was terrified of, with a social worker who hated foster children. But Nicole remained unaware. Clad in yellow corduroys and matching jacket and bonnet, she recklessly mounted her bike and rode face-into-the-wind in venturesome defiance. When Toni's sleek sports car drove up at exactly 10 A.M., I tried to smile for Nikki.

"Nikki, you are going for a bye-bye with this lady." I picked her up and headed for the car. Nikki looked around curiously and then studied me, her eyes skeptical with premonition. "Oh," I turned to Ms. Telford, "you don't have a car seat. I'll get ours."

"Don't bother. She'll be fine without one."

"I'll *get* the seat." Our verbal tug of war, had escalated into an undeclared war. "We just never permit our children to ride without car seats or seat belts," I explained as I brought out the car seat.

"Very well," she replied, "although it might be well to remember that Nicole is not your child."

I fastened Nikki into the car seat, kissed her on one pink cheek, willed back my tears; and waved.

As the car drove away she waved back and yelled, "Bye-bye, Mama. Nikki go bye-bye."

I went into the empty house, fixed myself some of my favorite tea, and let the tears flow. Nikki just said "Bye-bye" without any reluctance at all. I tried, with no success, to convince myself that it was because she was so secure, so well-adjusted, so loved, so trusting. But still I felt abandoned and betrayed.

All my good intentions for cleaning that day dissolved. Instead of working I chewed my fingernails to the quick, listened for the telephone, watched out the window, and cried—all at the same time, a kind of pat-your-stomach, rub-your-head exercise.

David called and we went out for lunch. But it seemed that everyone had a baby with them. At every baby noise, I was ready to respond. Being without the high chair, the chatter, and the crumbled crackers was intolerable.

"Let's get out of here," muttered David.

As we paid our check and walked out, I said, "There's no place to go, is there?"

And David, holding my hand, solemnly agreed. "No place at all."

David decided the office didn't need him so we went home, sipped coffee, and talked in sentences disjointed by time.

"David, it's two and she isn't here yet."

"Give it five minutes, Ann," he pleaded.

But soon we were both at the window watching every car that passed, willing the right one to appear. And when it finally did, it was David who reached the car first. Nikki screamed "Daddy" and collapsed sobbing into his arms.

I noticed that Nikki was dressed in a lightweight summer dress, sewn many years ago by someone who could not sew. "I put in extra corduroys," I explained.

"Well, they wanted to dress her up," Miss Telford explained. "In the future, please keep that in mind. Oh, she does have a bit of a scrape on her back where she fell off a swing. See you a week from today." She swung jauntily back to her car. I wondered how we'd suddenly gotten to weekly visits, but knew there was just one answer to that. Tilly the Hun was determined to make life as difficult for us as possible. Unfortunately, that included Nikki's life too.

"The Salvation Army wouldn't even accept this dress," David said as he began to undress the still-sobbing Nikki. "I thought that yellow corduroy outfit was new," he commented.

"It was," I cried as I pulled it from the diaper bag. "But that was before someone bleached it." I held up the useless garment for David to see.

"She didn't get this from a swing." David was examining

Nikki's scrape. "It looks more like a belt to me," he observed.

I looked too. It was not a scrape from a swing. I'd seen enough of them to know. From a belt? I couldn't tell.

We tucked Nikki into her favorite pajamas and took her to see Ben Lyons. He, too, was puzzled. "I don't think this happened accidentally. We'll take an x-ray although I don't expect to find anything." And he didn't. "These kinds of people know how to inflict an injury without leaving evidence," he added as we left. "It's almost an art with them. Unfortunately, what the courts want is irrefutable proof and that's death."

Laura had made macaroni and cheese ready for us when we reached home. Nikki alternately sobbed and crammed handfuls of her favorite casserole into her mouth. She discarded her spoon because it restricted her intake. In disbelief, David and I watched her eat. She obviously had not been fed all day. When she finished, Nikki announced firmly, "Bottle."

She hadn't asked for a bottle in months. David held her while she fell into a heavy sleep, consuming two full bottles in the process.

"David, what are we going to do?" I asked helplessly.

"I don't know," he replied. "She was hungry, injured, and exhausted. At least she'll probably sleep."

We had long been asleep, exhausted ourselves, when the howl began, a long, low cry like that of an animal alone in the wilderness, overcome with terror, estranged, in excruciating pain. When I reached her crib, Nikki was standing by the rail. I tried to pick her up to cuddle her, but she pushed me away and continued to moan. As David entered the room, her eyes turned to him. "Maybe she'll go to you; you didn't put her in that car."

But she rejected David too. Firmly, he picked her up and took her downstairs to her favorite rocking chair. I fixed another bottle, but she rejected it as well. David continued to hold her, alternately singing and making soothing noises. But Nikki was alone in a world of dark shadows that we could not dispel.

"You go to bed." David said. "You'll have this all day tomorrow." So I did, but I couldn't stop trembling with icy fear for a child, my child, who had to know such torture. And I felt overwhelming guilt at my inability to prevent this "abuse by consent of the agency."

"Mom, Dad, get up," Laura commanded. She had awakened at 5 A.M. and had taken over the early shift with Nicole. "Nikki just keeps biting herself and yelling, 'Bad baby'."

I reached for my robe and hurried down the stairs. Nikki was hitting herself clumsily as I picked her up.

"Good girl, Nikki. Mommy loves you. Daddy loves you. Everyone loves you." She looked at me with complete skepticism.

"I know, let's get dressed in the Raggedy Ann outfit." It was her favorite. I pulled off her pajamas and saw a multitude of self-inflicted bites on her arms. "Love, Nikki, love," I whispered softly as I kissed her wounds and dressed her.

She seemed distracted by a bowl of cereal, once again attacking her food animal-style, shoving in huge mouthfuls as though it might be her last meal.

After breakfast, I held Nikki while we read her favorite nursery rhymes. She settled peacefully onto my lap and was soon asleep.

When I laid her carefully in her crib, she sighed, a sigh I remembered from a much younger Nikki on a Christmas Eve many, many hurts ago. When would it ever end, I wondered.

"Alternatives? We have none," muttered Micah. "If we take them back to court on visits being detrimental, we'll lose for sure. Physical abuse doesn't count for much in the courts, and we'd get laughed out on psychological abuse. However, there is a professor out at the college—Ph.D. in psychology—that my wife thinks is on target when it comes to kids. I'll make an appointment with him for you and David. I've never yet met a psychologist who knows a single fact for sure, but let's give it a try."

"In the meantime we have to stand by and see the person, the very being of a child, destroyed?" I stammered.

"Maybe the relatives will leave town again." he responded.

"No, they're home free, Micah, and they know it. By the way, should I report this to Tilly the Hun?"

"Sure, there's got to be a heart there somewhere, although no one has seen any evidence of it yet," he admitted.

Toni Telford listened to me with obvious disdain. "Don't you realize that Nicole has to adjust to her own home? Periods when she seems confused and difficult to reach are to be expected. The behavior you describe is entirely normal for a child in transition. But, of course, if you don't want to cooperate, we can always move her to another foster home."

"No," I said firmly. "We'll find a way, somehow."

"See you on Tuesday then," she replied.

CHAPTER · 15

"Dr. Richard Clayton," the sign on the door read. "Do we knock or just go in?" I asked David.

"I heard Micah say once that if his wife were ever given a secretary she wouldn't know what to do with one. So I don't suppose any of the professors have them. I guess we knock."

"Come in," called a friendly voice from behind the door.

We entered Dr. Clayton's closet-sized office, wall-to-wall with books, a large desk, two twenties-vintage hardback chairs, and one leaking beanbag chair. Student papers mottled with grades and comments were strewn everywhere.

Dr. Clayton rose to greet us. "Hi, I'm Dick. You must be the Johnstons." A kind, eager face smiled behind a curly, blond beard. "Find a place to sit," he challenged. We chose the hardback chairs.

"Susan Madison told me a little about your situation but I'd like to hear it all, from the beginning," he invited.

So David began our story as Dick sprawled out on the beanbag and listened without interruption.

When David finished, Dick commented, "We have physical, psychological, and agency abuse. And we can prove none of it. It doesn't do any good, I suppose, to tell you this is a classic case."

We both shook our heads.

"I'd like to see your little Nicole when she has recovered from her first visit but before the next one. Then I'd like to see her the day following the visit. That way I can observe any differences, both objectively and subjectively. I can't say it will do much good, but who knows? There are still a few of us around who are going to continue to fight for the best interests of the child, simply because it's a matter of justice."

"Do you have any suggestions to help us deal with her behavior after the visits?" I asked.

"You are doing all that can be done. Reassure her of your

love. Keep on understanding how much she hurts. Watch carefully for physical abuse and report it to your physician. I'd keep that worker out of it as much as possible," he advised.

The day I took Nikki to see Dick Clayton, she was her usual exuberant self. She took to him enthusiastically, first determining that his beard was real, much to Dick's discomfort. He coaxed, "Nikki, would you like to go to see some toys?"

"Sure thing," she answered, imitating Lisa's latest all-purpose phrase.

As they walked off together down the hall, Nikki turned and waved. "Bye-bye, Mama."

Once they left I moved to the beanbag chair where I spent a quiet hour writing to the Great Aunts. Evetually the door opened, and I was interrupted by a singing, "Hi, Mama" as Nikki flew into my arms spilling us both out of the beanbag chair.

Dick grinned. "You have a real extrovert here. If I'd kept her another hour she'd be running the department. We don't like to label children so young, but Nikki is an exceptionally bright little girl, very verbal and well coordinated. She has good self-identification and also identifies strongly with you. She really has no problems. Too bad adults seem intent on creating them for her. Well, see you next Wednesday after the visit," he concluded.

"Bye, Dick," I said as we reached the door.

"Bye, Dick," repeated Nikki.

• • ● • •

Nikki was again ready at 10 A.M. for her visit. Spring was beginning to play hide-and-seek with winter, and Nikki's morning glories were beginning to peer from under the fallen leaves. Together we counted them. "Five, Mama, five," Nikki shouted.

I greeted Toni, car seat in hand, as she pulled up to the curb. She put the car seat into the car and reached for Nikki. But Nikki clung to me fearfully. "No, no," she screamed, surrendering herself to heartrending sobs.

Toni Telford got out of the car, walked resolutely around to the passenger side, and attempted to remove Nicole from my arms. Nikki hung on with all her strength even as I let my arms drop. "Mama, Mama," she sobbed.

"You'll have to take her; I won't push her away," I stated with firmness I didn't feel.

"Very well." She pried Nicole's tiny fingers from my neck, took her to the car, and buckled her into the car seat. "Mama, Mama," Nikki sobbed and reached out her arms to me. Toni reached over Nikki to slam the door. Long after the car had faded into the distance, all I could hear was "Mama, Mama."

Doing our income tax I decided would keep me busy without any emotional involvement. But later, when checking it, David would laugh until he rolled off the couch. "How could we possibly get a $3500 refund?" he would try to say through gasps of laughter. "You forgot decimal points. It should be thirty-five dollars."

"Laugh all you want," I would sputter. "There are people in this household who would never even have remembered we had to pay taxes." And to be absolutely sure that he would know who, I would put an ice cube down his collar.

But all that would happen much later. Right now I was awaiting Nikki's return with resolute calm. When I finished doing taxes, I burned some snicker-doodles and told myself that's why I was crying.

At two o'clock, as the car stopped at the curb, I restrained myself and let Toni bring Nikki to the door. As I opened it, Nikki flew into my arms, crying hysterically. "Go way, go way," she motioned to Toni.

As I held Nikki close I thought, I tried that approach too, but Tilly the Hun doesn't disappear with our brand of magic wands.

"I would like to come in, if you don't mind, Mrs. Johnston."

"Well, Nikki is upset and she needs a bath . . ."

"I won't be long. These short visits are difficult for Nikki so next week I'll pick her up on Tuesday and return her on Friday," she announced.

As Nikki sat, still sobbing in my arms, I protested, "If Nikki can't adjust during a short visit, how can a long one possibly be beneficial? Besides she's never been away from us overnight. Think how frightened a child not quite two would be if she awoke in the night in a strange environment."

"That environment is her real home. She loves it there." She smiled as she reached the door, "See you, Nikki."

I gazed at the small, tear-stained child in my lap, clutching me. Suddenly I was gripped by panic and submerged in hopelessness.

As I undressed Nikki for her bath, she trembled, her face still filled with fear. "Come on, Nikki. Let's go find the bubbles."

She followed me down the hall to the bathroom, shoulders slumped in defeat, a tiny figure of desolation, a shadow child.

When David arrived home, Nikki was warmly tucked into her pajamas and consuming copious quantities of spaghetti liberally laced with applesauce.

"Same story?" he asked.

"Worse. Next week she's going from Tuesday until Friday."

"Not if I can help it," David stormed. "Why can't these people see what's happening to this child?"

"I've thought about that a lot, David, and they don't want to see. There is no other explanation. Because if they really

116

wanted to see, they might have to act, and they might even have to make decisions for the child. And the agency isn't prepared to do that and then accept the consequences."

"You *are* taking Nikki to see Dick tomorrow?"

"Of course," I replied. "But sometimes I just get so tired, so fatigued emotionally. . ."

"I know," he said. "And the older kids know that too. They have the Nikki detail set up. They will take turns caring for her tonight."

"But she's our responsibility," I protested.

"They are very nearly adults, Ann. Don't measure their love for Nikki by the years they have lived," he admonished.

And so that night Laura, Lisa, and Matt took turns holding and comforting Nikki while I lay in bed, bone weary, longing for sleep, hearing Nikki's cry and knowing there was neither sleep nor peace for any of us.

· · ● · ·

It was an act of pure will to get an exhausted child and an equally exhausted mother to a psychologist. What were we trying to prove anyway? And if we could prove it, what difference would it make? Did I think Tilly the Hun would accept any opinion other than her own? Questions raced and collided in my tired brain, and I hoped I would not be stopped by the highway patrol and cited for confusion.

Nikki, sitting beside me, babbled in baby words. It took some time for me to realize that a regression in vocabulary was occuring.

My fears were confirmed by Dick. Nikki would not go with him to the toy room; instead she clung to me and hid her head. We finally went together to the testing area. Surrounded by every toy imaginable, Nikki still sat on my lap, security taking precedence over curiosity.

117

Dick coaxed her with a doll, cuddling it in his arms and then holding it out to Nikki. "Bad baby," she muttered as she slapped at the doll, refusing to take it.

Was this the same child who so lovingly cared for her dolls at home, tucking them carefully into their beds and attending to their every need? Or had that child disappeared forever, lost in a desolate figure of defeat? And could she ever again be found?

Leaving Dick's office, I stopped to call David. "Dick will support us all the way on doing something about these traumatic visits. He suggested that we go to the director of the welfare department, since Tilly has refused to help."

"All right," David agreed. "Meet you in half an hour at Child Abusive Services," he added.

· · • · ·

The welfare director sat pretzeled in his chair in a rumpled gray suit, his belly overlapping his beltless pants. His drooping, clay-colored face seemed frozen into a scowl. As we entered he set a half-eaten chili dog on a tomato-soaked paper napkin and perfunctorily waved us into black plastic chairs. I felt a wave of nausea and a strong desire to wash my hands.

As David tried to explain about Nicole, he waved his hand to stop him. "Know all about the case. The kid needs to go back to her mother. Go home and worry about your own family."

I protested. "But a child psychologist and our pediatrician are in strong agreement that these visits are detrimental to her best interests."

"My dear Mrs. Johnston, don't you know that the only place for a child is with his very own parents? Surely you

118

wouldn't want to have your own children taken from you to be raised by strangers?"

"Of course not, but *I* don't beat them, either. And besides, who *is* a stranger—the person who loves the child and cares for her as his own or blood relatives who cannot treat the child properly and whom the child fears?"

David added, "After a child has been in one home for nearly two years, where *is* her family? I happen to think it's with the people who love and care for her even if they don't share some blood relationship. Or are you one of those blood-is-thicker-than-love proponents?"

"My task is to reunite families. Now all of these families might not be as perfect as yours, Mr. and Mrs. Johnston, but they are families. If we always left the child where she wanted to be, we'd have an awful mess." He stifled a belch. "I'll have to ask you to leave now. I've important things to do. But if you have any more of these little problems, just take them to Miss Telford. After all it is her case."

In that moment David and I gave up on the system.

And in the following days Nikki slipped farther and farther from us. She became a shadow, darting among us, striving futilely to hide, needing to be comforted, unable to accept it. And yet we kept searching, kept reaching, for somewhere beyond this shadow child was our Nikki.

CHAPTER · 16

As I packed Nikki's clothes for her visit, each article of clothing brought back memories and evoked tears. Should I pack summer clothes or winter clothes? It was April and California weather could be unpredictable. Finally, I packed clothes for all seasons just to be safe.

Micah had called earlier, dismayed, defeated. He'd talked to Judge Anderson about the detrimental effect the visits were having on Nikki. He'd presented Dick's report which the judge had refused to read. Instead, Micah had gotten a stern lecture about reunification of child and family.

I wondered how the judge and county could view the natural family as they did. It seemed as if they saw each child as a missing piece in a puzzle and once the child was forced into that puzzle, she would automatically change the puzzle from a disorganized jumble into a masterpiece. If, by some chance, the child would not fit, she would be bent and molded, conformed, so that it appeared that she did.

When the doorbell rang, my heart fluttered. Tilly the Hun must be early. But when I opened the door, I saw that it was our priest, young, newly-ordained, and looking quite uncomfortable at the prospect of a home call. As he entered he announced, "I thought I'd say a blessing for your little one as she leaves on her journey." He stammered, "She *has* been baptized?"

I shook my head. "We asked a long time ago and we were told that she had not been and that we could not have it done."

Theological wrath aroused, he frowned in disbelief. "To baptize Nicole would, for me, be an act of nonviolent protest against the involvement of the state in religion."

Had David or I ever been that young, that naive, I wondered?

"But, you see, the reason we can't have her baptized isn't

theological conflict, it's the fact that we're not really her parents."

"*That* is not true. There's more to being a parent than giving birth," he stated flatly. He turned to me. "Go get the child," he ordered.

I dressed Nikki quickly in the strawberry-colored dress she'd worn on Easter. She clung to me, unwilling to be dressed, unwilling to face the unknown. I held her close, reassuring her as we descended the stairs.

Father Bryant used the simple service of baptism, the one reserved for times of crises. Nicole smiled shyly as she felt the holy water on her head and retraced the sign of the cross with her chubby fingers.

We had just finished when the doorbell rang. This time it *was* Ms. Telford. Nikki began screaming at as soon as Toni stepped into the room. When I introduced her as Nikki's social worker, Father Bryant looked bewildered. Still in reckless and rebellious spirit he asked, "If you represent the child, why does she become so hysterical at the sight of you?"

She answered, her voice edged with hostility, "The child is merely adjusting to her own home."

"If that 'home' were truly hers, she wouldn't be reacting this way," he protested.

"I have my job to do," she retorted, "just as you have yours."

"And if I did *my* job the way you do yours, I'd have twelve minutes—ten to pack and two to get out of town," he responded.

"We all see things in a different perspective."

"And what about this child? Perhaps she sees it in the most unobscured perspective of all. Her mind is unlittered by every law but the law of love."

She ignored him and turned to me. "Where is Nikki's suitcase?"

I pointed to the stairs, unable to speak. She picked up the

suitcase and pried Nikki from my arms. Father Bryant saw them to the car. I sat on the bottom stair where Nikki's suitcase had been and cried until there were no more tears.

The rest of the day passed vacantly. I tried mentally to reach out to Nikki, but there was no one there. That was day one.

On day two, David and I went shopping. I bought Nikki's summer clothes: three dainty sundresses, some shorts and matching shirts, a new swimming suit. I smiled to myself as I remembered her yelling "Here come," as she had dived into the pool. I was reaching for the good times and collecting mental blisters from hanging on.

On the third day I painted Nikki's crib a soft pink and papered her room with happy little girls clutching balloons. I washed all of Nikki's clothes and folded them carefully, treasuring memories.

Finally, it was Saturday. I heard David downstairs fumbling with the coffee maker, but I didn't join him for a round of "What If." The game went something like this: I'd say, "The mother and grandmother disappeared once, what if they should take Nikki and leave town?" David would reassure me, but his eyes betrayed him. He, too, was afraid we might not see Nikki again.

But promptly at 10 A.M. Tilly the Hun arrived at the door carrying Nikki in her arms. Nikki stretched out her arms weakly and, as David quickly took her, she slumped against his shoulder.

"Nikki is ill," Tilly announced. "You," she turned to me, speaking in scathing tones, "did not send appropriate clothing. The weather is extremely chilly, and you sent only summer clothing."

"I sent *both* summer and winter clothing because the weather *is* so unpredictable."

"Open the suitcase, Mrs. Johnston," she commanded.

With clammy hands shaking in premonition, I obeyed.

123

There were two little sundresses in the case and one disposable diaper.

"But I sent two little knit suits," I said. Turning to David I pleaded for response, "You remember, the little checked ones? One was green and the other was blue."

He nodded.

"And I sent four corduroy one-piece playsuits with long sleeves. Nikki wore them all winter so they were not new, but they were still warm. And I sent her little yellow, fuzzy winter jacket. Impulsively I turned to Miss Telford. "You remember, she had on a pink dress when you took her—where is that?" I demanded.

"How could I possibly remember what she was wearing? I have only two very differing sets of facts and a very sick child. Can you prove you sent those things?"

Helplessly, I admitted that I had packed Nikki's things myself and that no one else had seen them.

David spoke angrily. "I didn't see the clothes packed, but if my wife says she sent them, she did."

"Sometimes we live with a person for years and never really know them," Toni sympathized.

"And some people cannot recognize the truth when it meets them on a clear day! Now if you want to make a charge against my wife, just be sure you have the evidence. Otherwise, I'd suggest you let us get Nicole to the doctor."

"Of course," she replied. "Only this time place the blame where it belongs."

When she was gone, I sat head buried in my hands, while David, balancing Nikki, called Dr. Lyons. "I'll take her in," he decided.

"David, I guess I must be really naive. I never thought I'd need proof of the type of clothing I sent."

"I know," he muttered. "It seems we can never run fast enough, let alone get ahead of them."

David left with Nikki, but I already knew she had

pneumonia and that the blame was going to be mine and that there was nothing, no evidence, to clear me.

Impulsively I called Greg Adams and related the story to him. "It makes no sense except as a frame to get the case back to court for a special hearing," Greg responded. "Nicole's relatives don't have the brains to concoct this. Rolich instructed them; you can be sure of that. I'm sorry I ever got you people into all of this."

"She's worth it, Greg, whatever the price, whatever the sorrow," I concluded. "David's back," I announced. "See you," I dismissed him as I hung up.

David strode in carrying a feverish, but sleeping Nicole. "Pneumonia," he announced.

"Poor little girl," I sympathized as I took her. "David, I did pack those clothes. What if no one believes me?"

"Of course, you did," David reassured me. "Ben says Rolich uses this kind of thing frequently."

"Ben believed me, didn't he?" I faltered.

"Sure he did. He said that you shouldn't blame yourself. It was entrapment, pure and simple. And if they couldn't do it with clothes, you can be certain that there were alternate plans."

"How can they even pretend to care for Nicole when they'd risk her well being in this manner?" But I knew the answer already. It was money, three hundred dollars a month to be exact. Property to be regained at all costs. A battle merely for the sake of battle. And none of it had anything to do with the small child who lay on my lap, breathing heavily, except that she was the pawn. And she didn't even want to play the game.

Nikki reached for my hand and held it to her hot cheek. She smiled softly and drifted into a wheezing sleep as I rocked her. I laid her gently in her newly-painted crib. Walls of bright balloons smiled around her, and Big Bear, perched in the corner of the crib, guarded her.

As I entered the kitchen, David was hanging up the

125

receiver. "Micah says it's a ploy to get the case back to court, just as Greg said."

"In January I thought we'd have Nicole for another whole year and that seemed like forever. And now forever may end today or tomorrow. I'm not ready."

"Well, it hasn't happened yet," David tried to reassure me.

· · ● · ·

But it did. Micah called to tell us a date for a special hearing had been set due to what was legally called a "change of circumstance." This time the county would be recommending that Nicole be returned to her mother and grandmother. David held me in his arms and we both sobbed, openly heartbroken.

There was just one weekend before the hearing. We had a few moments to heed the beckoning of the cottage, to seek reassurance and peacefulness from the sea.

CHAPTER · 17

Nikki bounced back from pneumonia like a rubber ball, so rapidly that I wondered how early a child could be victimized by his or her own psyche. Although we continued the antibiotic, we had to chase Nikki to give her medication, and then she'd smile and run away again, as if to tell us that the whole thing was unnecessary because she'd invented it.

Nikki had many secrets now, ones that she could not share. Often, thumb in mouth, she'd climb onto my lap and put her chubby arms around my neck, wanting to be consoled with stories and rhymes. She was fearful of going outside the house and terrified of the car. She wanted to restrict her world to familiar things and would let nothing new in unless it received her seal of security.

Yet the sea continued to beckon. As I packed our clothing Nikki's eyes grew fearful. "No, no," she pleaded, and promptly began to unpack the clothes.

"Nikki, remember the ocean and the beach," I prodded her. But Nikki remembered other things that went with suitcases, things I knew nothing about.

Finally, Laura rescued both Nikki and me and tucked Nikki into her stroller along with the tennis racquet and balls, and Nikki went along to referee the game.

"Mom, will we lose Nikki?" Lisa asked fearfully.

"I don't know," I replied. "We just have to hope that the judge has seen enough of Rolich's tactics to recognize what is happening," I replied.

"Well, can't we let someone search the house for Nikki's clothes and if they can't find them. . . ?" she proposed.

"Or get a search warrant for the grandmother's house?" Matt suggested hopefully.

"No, we have to remember that the clothes aren't really the issue. They've been waiting since last January to find an opportunity to get the case back to court. Micah thinks Rolich probably had several plans."

"Well, they don't treat Nikki right when they have her," Matt stormed. "I just don't understand why the judge doesn't sit everybody together and then let Nikki choose. She'd come to us right away."

"They do that, Matt, when they think a child has reached the age of reason, about twelve. Only the judge talks to the child."

Lisa was indignant. "What they are really saying then is that you can know about love only in your head."

"Just about, Lisa. Usually the court appoints an attorney for the child, but that attorney just reads the agency's recommendations and does what the agency wants. Usually, Micah says, they read it during court or just before like that Wallace person in the January hearing. It is a pretense of representation at best and downright deceptive at worst."

That weekend we drove to the place where sea and sand, seagulls and shells and cottage beckoned. Nikki laughed in greeting when she saw the cottage, and most certainly the cottage shouted a greeting in return.

We ran down the trail to greet the sea and it too roared a welcome. Nikki gurgled and grinned and ran for the sea. She stopped abruptly as a wave washed over her toes, then she raced back to me, arms outstretched. "Beach, Mama," she pointed.

"Do you like the beach, Nikki?" I asked, smiling at her enthusiasm.

She nodded affirmatively and mischievously raced off again yelling "Catch, catch."

David laughed and chased her down the beach, pretending to try so hard to catch her, but letting her run just ahead of him, in gleeful victory.

But I was remembering the other time, when it had been Nikki's first birthday and she and I had crept down to the beach shortly after dawn. That was the day when I had first made up the haunting rhyme:

> You ran away from Mama.
> You ran away from Dad.
> And Laura
> And Matthew
> And Lisa too.
> And no one can catch you,
> Not even Julie or Jill,
> Because you're our own Little Gingerbread Girl.

The poem still gripped me with its poignancy. Through tears I yelled, "David, catch her. Let's build a castle."

David caught Nikki and turned her upside down over his shoulder and galloped toward me grinning, while Nikki shrieked in delight.

We set to work on construction of the castle, and soon Jill and Julie joined us. We carefully dug little tunnels while Nikki piled sand in her pail and delivered it to the construction site. Eyes dancing merrily, she watched the castle near completion. At last David pulled a small car from his pocket and handed it to Nikki. "This year's model, designed especially for little girls with castles." Nikki carefully drove her car up the road we had built to the castle, over the roof, and in one window.

"There," she muttered in satisfaction. "Car go night-night." And then she raced for the sea, having disposed of such matters as sand castles and cars.

The wind brushed her curls until they stood high, and the sea nipped playfully at her toes. She turned to wave at us, smiling contentedly. Our Gingerbread Girl did not look to the future or dwell in the past. Today was forever and there was sea and surf and sand and sunshine and smiles. David reached for my hand and I knew we were sharing the same thought.

"I thought we could leave it all behind if we came here,"

he said thoughtfully, "but we can't. Nikki did though. She lived each day for itself. Her whole life was bounded by the things that count. Tomorrow wasn't even a possibility for her. And yesterday no longer existed."

The courtroom had lost none of its drab, despairing look. Even in late spring the chill lingered. Gloom crept up one aisle and down the next. I longed for the Great Aunts (who had taken a trip to Portugal, a pre-season special). I longed for the children and for every friendly face I'd ever known. I wished they would fill the courtroom so the intolerable, gripping fear would be outnumbered and would disappear, never to be experienced again. But it was not to be. Fear knew this place as its own, and it claimed me with a firm grip, chaining me, throbbing within me. Even David looked strained, and I knew he too had lost the war with fear.

That day I'd packed the suitcase, why didn't I know it was momentous, that it was a day I would need a witness to every activity? But Micah had said it would not have mattered, that we would have needed a witness to *all* things, a continuous video tape of our lives. From the moment of the last hearing, we had needed proof, he said, of our right to exist. Existence to me had always been a matter of faith in the past. Now it had become a matter of hard proof. It's one thing to take Kierkegaard's leap of faith: it's quite another to take a leap of proof—if you jump without a backpack full of irrefutable evidence, you've jumped into a bottomless pit.

Tilly the Hun entered the courtroom balancing expertly on three-inch heels, her head held high in the spirit of the righteous. Shirk ambling in after her wore his familiar brown tweed suit and scuffed penny loafers. Apparently he was through making "statements."

The parade continued as Nicole's mother and grandmother strode smugly toward seats in the front of the courtroom. Then Harvey Rolich appeared—so bouyantly triumphant I half-expected ticker tape to shower down from the chandeliers. He shook hands cordially with Dennis Shirk, then embraced Tilly the Hun and roared his approval at some comment she made.

Loneliness settled with certainty on David and me. Hands interlocked, fingers clasped, we clung to each other for protection. We were lost together in a nightmare of fear.

Micah arrived, waved a greeting, opened his briefcase, and was lost in concentration. Only yesterday he had said, "We have to raise a reasonable doubt in Anderson's mind about the visits. Unless we can do that, we are not likely to win."

But what constitutes reasonable doubt, I wondered. A child who becomes hysterical and yells both before and after visits? A child who becomes dependent and fearful? Unfortunately, it would take a reasonable person to admit the possibility of reasonable doubt. I recalled Caroline's assessment of Judge Anderson. "But later when it really counts he's just like the rest of them, equates the family with patriotism and Americanism and refuses to be educated."

I thought of the clipping I had received from Caroline after the last hearing. "Ann, dear, you must have this. It is the editorial in the local press written when your grandfather died. He was the kind of man who would have heard Nikki's case with fairness."

I read and reread the editorial until it became a part of me:

> "Judge Albert never occupied the seats of the mighty and never aspired to, but in his own immediate milieu he was a man of parts and the possessor of a shrewd common sense that made him a man worth one's while to talk to. Although long a citizen of here none ever accused him of meanness, ignobility, nor deceit. He had the courage of his convictions and was unafraid to take an unpopular stand. His knowledge of law was tempered with the wisdom of consequences. He was of the fine moral fiber that the best Americanism is built from."

I swallowed a sob, longing for that kind of justice for Nikki.

And then the bailiff entered. "All stand," he intoned. "Superior Court, State of California, County of Apthorp now in session. Judge Dwight Anderson presiding."

"The matter before the court," Judge Anderson announced, "is a special hearing for Nicole Russell. Are all the parties ready?" Each attorney nodded affirmatively. Shirk turned to look at us, then at Micah. He appeared to be somewhat bewildered.

"Mr. Shirk, please proceed."

Shirk hesitated, then stood. "The county recommends that the child remain in the Johnston home until the next annual review."

Toni and Rolich sprang to their feet in protest. Acknowledging them, Judge Anderson intoned, "Since there seems to be opposition to Mr. Shirk's recommendation, I'm calling a five-minute recess so that Mr. Shirk can be apprised of the position of his client."

Micah, grinning, strode over to us. "Well, Shirk's instincts are right. Too bad he wasn't permitted to proceed. We'd have unusual grounds for an appeal."

But the hearing went on with only Micah arguing for Nicole to remain in our home. This time it was Tilly the Hun who took the stand first.

She spoke glowingly about the preservation of the family, the love of the mother and grandmother for Nicole, and Nicole's love for them. She reported that the visits had been successful. "The real problem at the moment is the foster parents. They are uncooperative. In fact, in preparing for the last visit, the foster mother packed only summer clothing for the child. As a result, the child contracted pneumonia. It is time for the child to be returned to the environment in which she belongs, with people who are relatives, who love her, who can care for her," she concluded.

Micah was the only attorney who rose to examine the witness.

133

"Miss Telford, you speak of Nicole's love for her family. Tell me, is hysterical crying an indication of *love?*" he asked.

"She does cry, but I'm convinced that she cries because she does not want to leave her mother and grandmother to return to the foster home."

"Come now, Miss Telford, does that really make sense? We have here affidavits from a pediatrician, a psychologist, and the former worker all contrasting Nicole's behavior before and after visits. Before visits she was a happy, carefree, bright child. After the visits, she was hysterical and fearful, and had a loss of communicative skills. How do you explain that? "

She replied, "First of all, Nicole is extremely overprotected in the foster home. As for these affidavits, they're useless. These people have probably been paid to have opinions favorable to the foster parents."

"Would you like to make a formal charge against Ben Lyons, Richard Clayton, and Greg Adams? Your allegations are extremely serious."

She tossed her head. "You know as well as I do that people form the opinions they are told to form."

"No, I don't know that," replied Micah. "It might come as a surprise to you that many people still feel that integrity is of the highest order and that they are bound by whatever demands it imposes." Changing course abruptly, Micah asked, "Did you personally see the clothes that were packed for the child during the last visit?"

"No," she admitted.

"You did not check the suitcase yourself either at the foster home or at the home of the natural parent before the visit?"

"No."

"Well, then, how did you form the conclusion that the appropriate clothes were not packed in the suitcase?" Micah inquired.

134

"Because I *did* see the clothes at both homes following the visit," she affirmed.

"Isn't it possible that the clothes were packed and subsequently removed by the relatives?"

"Objection, your honor. Mr. Madison is impugning the integrity of my clients." Rolich stormed.

"Sustained. And Mr. Madison, I fail to follow this line of questioning at all. Can you enlighten me?" Judge Anderson inquired.

"There is a question here of whether appropriate clothing was provided during a visit. The child subsequently developed pneumonia, and it is essential to my case to prove that there is no third party, no impartial witness, to prove that the foster parents did not provide the proper clothing for the visit."

"I am going to rule that this line of questioning is irrelevant to the case. We are here to determine if the rehabilitative process is sufficiently complete for the child to be returned home." Anderson spoke firmly. "As for these affidavits, Mr. Madison, I am inclined to accept Miss Telford's explanation that solicited opinions are not impartial."

"Your honor," Micah protested, "this hearing was called because of a debate about proper clothing."

"There is no mention of that except as supporting evidence, Mr. Madison. We are not going to take the court's time to discuss what a two-year-old wears. There is just one question before this court and that is, can this child be returned to her family," Anderson admonished.

Micah sighed. "No more questions."

David and I looked at each other hopelessly. Apparently, the clothing issue was important enough to get us back into court, but not important enough to discuss once we got there. It was incomprehensible.

Mr. Rolich stood. "I have no more questions for this witness, your honor, but I would like to commend her on her courage and forthrightness." As Tilly stepped down, he assisted her from the witness box with exaggerated gallantry.

"Mr. Shirk, do you have any other witnesses?"

Shirk, questioningly, turned to Tilly the Hun who shook her head vehemently.

"Mr. Rolich?" the judge turned to the relative's counsel.

"I'd like to call the grandmother, Mrs. Russell," and he turned to assist her down the aisle.

"Now, Mrs. Russell, I know how many tears you have shed for your granddaughter. Please try not to cry now. Be brave for little Nicole's sake," he sympathized. "Now will you try?"

"Yes," she answered in her harsh, gravelly voice.

"Now, in your own words, tell me about your visits with Nicole."

"Oh, she loves us so. That little one can hardly wait to get to our home. And how we miss her when she leaves. Oh, I can't tell you, Mr. Rolich, what it is like to have your own grandaughter living with strangers and knowing they don't even put the right kind of clothes on her to fit the weather. I tell you only God can be protecting her. I can't go on!"

"I'm finished, your honor," Rolich asserted.

"I have some questions, your honor." Micah arose. "According to the mental health report, you and your daughter have been to mental health once during the past eighteen months. Yet this is part of the rehabilitation agreement. How do you expect to have the child returned to you when you have not complied with the agreement?"

Helen Russell turned to Harvey Rolich, "He's calling me crazy, isn't he?" and she burst into tears.

"David," I whispered, "we aren't going to win, are we?"

"It really looks bad," he admitted.

Micah turned to Judge Anderson. "If this witness is not prepared to answer questions, then I ask that the court adjourn until she is prepared to continue. I asked a legitimate question regarding the rehabilitation agreement and I would like an answer."

Rolich rose in indignation. "This woman is a poor grandmother, deprived of her only grandchild, upset and disturbed by the insinuations of counsel. This is a simple woman who lives a simple life. She cannot be expected to answer questions she cannot understand. As for the agreement to attend mental health therapy, I understand that the county has rescinded that agreement in view of the obvious stability of the mother and grandmother."

Tilly the Hun nodded in agreement.

"Mr. Madison, stop badgering this witness and I'm certain that she can continue," Anderson commanded.

"No more questions," Micah sighed.

"Any additional witnesses, Mr. Rolich?" Anderson inquired.

"No, the dear little mother, Marilyn, wants her child back, but she is so fearful of opposing counsel that I am not going to put her on the stand."

David whispered to me, "Naturally not. She destroyed his case last time. She doesn't want Nicole back."

"Very well. You may call your witnesses, Mr. Madison," the judge frowned at Micah.

"I call the foster father, David Johnston." David looked mildly surprised. I breathed a sigh of relief. We had been certain that I would be called first again.

"Mr. Johnston, I want you to explain how Nicole acted after visits with her relatives," Micah urged.

David explained matter-of-factly about how we had stayed up all night with her, how frightened she was and how hysterical she became.

"And what is Nicole's usual behavior?"

"She is a happy child, loving and carefree. These visits produce a complete change of personality, one that seems to be cumulative in destructiveness." David answered.

"Mr. Rolich has inferred that these personality changes

137

are the result of the child's longing for the mother and the grandmother," Micah stated.

"That can't possibly be true. During the months when no visits occurred, Nicole was very happy and her development was quite accelerated. It was only when the visits began to take place again that she became unhappy and frightened."

"Your witness, Mr. Rolich," finished Micah.

"Is it not true, Mr. Johnston, that you wish to adopt Nicole?" Rolich demanded.

"Yes, now that it is apparent that her relatives cannot care for her," David asserted.

From the back of the room came a wail from the grandmother. "Our baby, our baby, that man is stealing our baby!"

The gavel fell as Anderson spoke. "Mr. Rolich, I realize that this is a very sensitive issue, but you must control your client."

"May I have a five-minute recess? We always suspected that these people were trying to snatch little Nicole; now we have the foster father's own testimony. You certainly must forgive a display of emotion in such circumstances." Rolich demanded.

"Five minutes," Judge Anderson replied wearily.

Micah motioned us out of the room. "We're going to lose her, aren't we?" I asked fearfully.

"We lost a lot when Child Protective Services reneged on its demand for mental health. Now, basically, they have met the terms of rehabilitation."

"And it doesn't matter how Nikki reacts or feels, does it?" I asked.

"No," Micah replied. "We lost any concern for Nicole's welfare when Tilly the Hun became the caseworker."

Five minutes isn't a very long time when the life of a child is at stake. I wanted to run from the courtroom, take Nikki, and keep running.

I was called next by Micah. He hadn't given up. "Mrs.

Johnston, tell me about your meeting with Richard Clayton, the psychologist at the college."

"Objection!" Rolich screamed.

"The witness is merely reporting something that happened to her," Micah defended.

"Very well, Mr. Madison, you may go on. Since you seem determined to get this irrelevant material into the record, we may as well listen or we'll be here all year."

Micah nodded at me to proceed.

"I took Nicole to Dr. Clayton twice, once at a period between visits and once immediately following a visit. During the first appointment she was easily tested and during the second, she was so fearful that she could not be tested. The difference in circumstances was also reflected in her performance. The first visit revealed that she was a bright, well-adjusted child. The second visit proved her to be insecure and developmentally regressive."

Rolich rose with deliberate menace. "I move that this be stricken from the record as irrelevant. It is based on subjective observation from a family that has admitted to wanting to snatch the child."

"Sustained." Judge Anderson gave no explanation.

"An affidavit has been submitted to the court from Dr. Clayton corroborating this witness's statements," Micah protested. "And, before Mr. Rolich objects, let me also state that there was no charge for the psychological testing for Nicole."

"Now can we please get to final summations?" Anderson appealed. "And I don't want to hear anymore about who packed what clothing."

A cold inevitability overcame me. I knew there was no more to be done.

Micah too seemed to realize that no one was going to listen to Nicole's voice, that in their ears her opinion had no merit—not even when that opinion concerned her very existence.

In defeat, Micah dismissed me from the witness box.

"Any other witnesses?" Anderson asked abruptly.

"No, your honor," Micah answered. As he told us later, God Himself wouldn't have been heard in that kangaroo court.

"Then, let's try to keep the final summations brief and to the point," Anderson commanded. "Mr. Shirk, you may proceed."

"Yes, your honor. Even though the county recommended that this child remain in foster care at the Johnston's that was when there was a different worker for the case who was fearful that the child would again be injured." Tilly the Hun looked ready to fly again. "Now we are recommending that the child be returned to her mother and grandmother." He stopped, looked doubtful, and turned to Tilly for reassurance. She nodded, "Miss Telford claims that these visits went well, although Mr. Madison, whom I deeply respect, disagrees. Well, anyway, the county recommends that the child be returned to her relatives." He sat down with obvious discomfiture.

"Mr. Rolich," Anderson muttered.

Rolich rose in triumph, turning to reassure the Russells. "We have here a case of grave injustice in which three innocent people have been caught—three generations, a grandmother, a mother, and a child. Look at those people. Would they harm a child? Of course not. No, they were victims themselves. And so was the child. She was not cared for properly. And she came to every visit screaming to get away from that home. I ask now that the previous injustices be rectified and that the child be returned to her home thirty minutes following the hearing."

The tears were rolling down my cheeks, and a sob threatened to choke me. How could facts be so distorted?

"Mr. Madison," the judge indicated with a nod.

"Your honor, we have here some flagrant departures from fact. First of all the foster parents took this child when she was beaten, undernourished, and emotionally deprived. With love and care, she has become a bright, loving, healthy child.

"Visits from her natural parents have been extremely detrimental to her well-being. We have presented adequate evidence of that from both foster parents, her former worker, and Drs. Clayton and Lyons. Even if only a reasonable doubt exists, can the life of a child be risked? But, in this case, we have more than reasonable doubt. We have irrefutable proof that the child is terrified of her relatives. Before a child can be returned to a home, it seems that the reasons behind her behavior in the presence of her relatives need to be ascertained. Then I would have liked to implement the plan for mental health rehabilitation. Do these people seem like stable people? I think we have ample evidence of that instability in their behavior today. The grandmother was nearly incoherent and the mother could not testify at all." He paused.

"It is against all logic, all common sense, to return this child to her relatives. In what way are circumstances any different for the Russells than on the day that Nicole was removed? In eighteen months, they have seen the child five times. Five times," he repeated, "and five traumas for the child. One worker was abruptly taken from the case because his conscience would not allow him to permit his own agency to continue to abuse the child. There are, in fact, two kinds of abuse here: the actual abuse which resulted in the removal of the child from her home—abuse, I might add, that was substantiated at the detention hearing in February. And, second, we have an even more flagrant abuse—abuse by consent of the agency, the very agency that was designated to protect the child. This baby of two years of age is the victim of abuse by the system, an indictment of unimaginable circumstances."

He continued, "Did *anyone* listen to the testimony of the foster parents which was corroborated by a psychologist and a pediatrician? I repeat, this child is terrified of her relatives. She will not eat when she visits them. She has long episodes of hysteria following visits. We know that there are two million cases of child abuse in the United States each year. Last year Nicole was one of them. We also know that there are ten thousand reported cases of death from child abuse each year. If Nicole is returned to that home, she could well be numbered among that statistic too. Children do die in their own homes at the hands of their own parents. Sometimes it just happens and we can do nothing. Other times, we are given the opportunity to prevent it. Today is one of those times. Reason dictates that it is in the best interests of the child to continue to protect her. Her very life may depend upon the decision made in this courtroom today." Clearly Micah was engulfed in deep mental anguish as he finished, pleading, "Leave the child where she is loved and protected."

Anderson did not even hesitate. Afterward we heard that these decisions are often made in advance and not even in the guise of such high-minded ideals as the protection of the family. Judicial decisions are for sale, often at bargain prices. But then we strained to hear every word. "It has been apparent since the beginning of this special hearing that there could be only one decision made. By every moral law this child belongs to her own mother and grandmother and as of thirty minutes from now they will assume complete custody of her. Case dismissed."

Thirty minutes. I could not believe my ears. Thirty minutes to say goodbye for a lifetime, thirty minutes to love. Both David and I, stunned and blinded with tears, were led from the courtroom by Micah. He assured us, "I'll start working on an appeal immediately. Ann, you are just losing her for a little while."

Around us, everyone else was jubilantly and boisterously claiming victory.

As David and I, arm in arm, began to leave, Tilly yelled, "Have her ready when I get there."

I opened drawers and carelessly stuffed the accumulation of two years of life into large plastic bags while David held Nicole and dialed the schools to have the children sent home to say goodbye. Nicole laughed and giggled as he tickled her—one last time. As the older children straggled in, dismayed and tearful, they took turns holding Nikki, hugging her and cherishing her—one last time. And Nikki, who could not know, responded to all the attention with smiles and laughter and her newest words, "Nikki happy, happy, happy."

When the doorbell rang and Tilly entered, Nikki's smiles dissolved into tears, her laughter to screams of terror. Tilly walked straight to Nikki and, without a word, picked her up, ignoring Nikki's screaming and kicking. "No, no, no," were the last words I heard as Tilly strode out the door, followed by David and Matt carrying bags of clothing and toys.

"Goodbye, little Gingerbread Girl," I whispered to myself. "Goodbye." And then I cried.

CHAPTER · 19

David and I had always thought we could endure anything in life except losing each other or one of the children. And now we knew the stark reality of that. There was not an hour of the day when I did not reach out for Nikki. We found small evidences of her everywhere, a forgotten toy, an undershirt, a small ball, a book.

At the grocery store, as I passed the baby section, I had to leave a cart of groceries and give way to loud, uncontrollable sobs.

David too said he knew what it was to push papers. His faithful secretary shouldered most of the work, understanding that grief demands its own priorities and its own moment.

Even meals became painful. Absently, I asked Laura to dish up Nikki's spaghetti first so that it would cool. "Nikki doesn't live here anymore," she cried as she ran to her room.

Nikki was everywhere and nowhere. What was she doing now, this moment? Was there anyone to feed her? Would she eat? I had learned now that what pediatricians tell mothers is not true—that a child will not starve if adequate food is provided. That premise was correct only if the child was in a loving, caring environment. Nikki had literally starved herself as an infant and later she returned from visits gulping food in unbelievable amounts. Nikki was fully capable of using food as a weapon of defiance, as one of her few effective weapons.

· · ● · ·

We tried to go on because life requires that. The world doesn't make accomodations for grief. Life goes on and demands that we go with it; no one sits out ineligible for play.

So we went to the market and were stopped by a police car. "You don't have a current license on your car," the patrolman noted.

"License?" David faltered as though he had never heard of such a thing.

"Yes, sir. May I see your driver's license?" the officer inquired suspiciously.

I stared back, screaming inwardly, *We lost a child; that's our world and our reality. We don't live in your world anymore!*

But we got the ticket. The world demanded conformity. My mind jumped back to the days of teaching. "David, we're out of compliance." And I giggled hysterically into sobs.

Second notices arrived on bills and third notices and final notices. And none of it meant anything. We had lost a child. Time out, world. Pléase stop. Listen. We have lost a child. But someone seemed to say, "No, Ann, you may not be excused from living." The bills still came, the telephone still rang, and my family still wanted to eat.

"Let grief have its moment," I had written when I was very wise. But now, blessed by ignorance again, I knew that no one was ever going to give me a moment alone with grief. So I went on playing the game, juggling grief in whatever way I could.

Some friends, trying to help, called to say they didn't know what to say. "Just say you're sorry," I wanted to scream. "Say that you love us and that you want us to get well. Can't you even say that?" Other friends stayed away because grief is difficult to talk about and impossible to share. There even seemed to be a fear of contagion. It would be easier to say, later, that they would have helped if they had known. And how could they possibly have known when their own kitchen floor needed scrubbing, the car needed to be waxed, and Janie needed braces on her teeth?

We lived alone in those days in a world embarrassed by grief, in a world that denied the reality of loss.

Even at church, although the congregation remembered us in prayers, friends pretended to forget after the service. It was an uncomfortable subject, one they might share with God, but not with us.

In those days I remembered Ben Lyons' stern admonition, "Do you know the heartbreak that inevitably accompanies these situations? Just remember that the court will rule for the natural parent in the face of all evidence to the contrary. . . . We can't change a society which really places very little value on the best interests of the child."

And I remembered some of Micah's words as he spoke of the charade of courts and judges and social workers and lawyers: "Society heaps abuse on children at the same time it alleges to rescue them. When a little child like your Nicole can find a home to call her own, that's where she ought to stay. . . . I try to see who the child is bonded to because that's where the best interests of the child are."

Nicole had found her home, her family, and she was taken from it harshly and with cruel haste. She was taken away from rocking chairs and morning glories, swimming pools and tennis matches, the sea and the sand, and a Mother and a Father and a Laura and a Lisa and a Matt and a Julie and a Jill.

· · ● · ·

In desperation, once, we drove by Nikki's house hoping to catch a glimpse of her—any glimpse that might indicate that she was still alive. But the shack where she had lived was empty, the front door sagging open and a sloppily printed "For Rent" sign propped against the splintered steps. Nikki and her family were gone.

Back home I called Greg at Child Protective Services. "Can't we even know if she's alive and well?" I asked.

"That information is so classified the President couldn't find out. In cases like this the child's file just disappears," he replied. "Let her go, Ann. You'll never see her again."

Then the phone calls began. A nurse from a nearby metropolitan hospital called. "Your baby was here. She'd been beaten badly, but it was all hushed up. I'd get fired if anyone knew I called you." David and I rushed to the hospital, but were met with cold indifference. No such child had ever been treated there.

Two weeks later the same nurse phoned again. "The baby was in again." Her voice broke. "She was beaten so badly— you have to do something."

We turned to Ben Lyons. Perhaps another doctor could find out what we could not. "Ann, I'm sorry," he commented when he called back. "I found out nothing."

"What do you think, Ben?" I asked. "Was it her?"

He sighed. "Neither of us will ever know."

And we did not. A little girl named Nikki had disappeared from the face of the earth. I watched for her in every crowd, and my heart would leap when I saw a tiny girl with brown curls and large brown eyes. But it was never Nicole.

A deep loss enveloped us. Sometimes we stepped carefully around emotion and at other times we plunged into it without restraint. There was an aching feeling that there would never again be happiness in our lives, as if our allotted joy had been consumed for a lifetime. The loss of a child is unlike any other experience; it leaves a gaping gash in the soul.

One day soon after we had lost Nikki, a package arrived in the mail. When I opened it, out tumbled one of Nikki's little dresses, all bloody and wrinkled, with the remains of a dandelion still in one pocket. The accompanying letter stated that the court was releasing all evidence in the case of Nicole Russell and that the case was now officially closed.

But I knew that for us it would never be closed. We would always listen for Nikki's footsteps, knowing that each day they would grow fainter. We would always wait for one child to catch up. Our lives had stopped in the midst of the laughter and tears of a two-year-old, and it seemed that nothing could ever again be quite the same. The rest of our lives we would always be looking back, yearning for a child we had loved and lost, a child forever beyond reach. I hugged the dress closely and wept.

EPILOGUE

Moments passed and eventually became days. Slowly reality became truth; Nikki was really gone. Eventually life swept us up and carried us along to new days Nikki would never know.

Micah ran for the State Assembly and won by the largest landslide in district history. With his wife and boys he moved to Sacramento where he authored legislation for children's rights in the face of federal legislation which, frequently at the expense of the child, gives first priority to the biological family. Rumor says that he still spends most of his spare moments at juvenile hall.

Greg Adams resigned from Child Protective Services and began work as an investigative reporter. His crusades are devastatingly direct and often aimed at his former employer. His forthright approach and detailed research attracts favorable attention in the literary world. Someday, I'm sure, the Pulitzer will be his.

Tilly the Hun received a promotion and became the director of Child Protective Services. It is said that she has the combination of administrative ability and the total lack of empathy for children that the job requires. She is now in a position to sanction the abuse of all children under the loving care of Child Protective Services. Few will ever learn that she, too, is a victim of the system, someone who also needs protection.

Judge Anderson continued to rule for the natural parents in the next sixteen consecutive cases before him. He then suffered a coronary and was forced to retire from the bench. He was replaced by a judge who continued to rule for the natural parent, a reasonable man, but swayed by outmoded ideas about the family, uneducated about the kind of society that exists today.

Laura went away to college to study pre-law, leaving the

house even more empty. By now Nikki's presence lingered only in moments of great joy or great pain. Sometimes in the middle of the night I thought I heard her scream, and once or twice I was sure I heard a whispered giggle. Overwhelmed by emptiness and loss, I found it easiest to just lie in bed or wander through the empty house. I prayed in desperation, "Lord, the burden is so heavy I can't manage." It was as though I'd somehow found the strength to help the others through and now that they were resuming their lives I'd lost the ability to cope with my own. Meals were either prepared haphazardly or not at all. Breakfast had been a special time for Nikki and me, a time to spend exploring the first fresh moments of each day. Now I did not get up until the last child had left for school.

The day of the first rain, tears oozed from the sky and I found myself walking listlessly to the window to watch the raindrops slide down the pane. As I stood there, a car stopped in front of the house and a woman emerged with an infant carrier. Dashing quickly to protect the baby from the rain, she approached the house and rang the doorbell.

Reluctantly I opened the door to a woman I had met at foster parent meetings. "May I come in?" Karen asked, and I realized I'd just been staring at her.

"Yes, of course," I stammered, moving back from the door so that she could enter.

"This is Holly," she said, indicating the small form in her arms. "She's a foster child from Homes for Children and is going to be adopted as soon as the agency frees her. I wonder if you would keep her for just a short time while my husband takes me out to lunch."

It wasn't a lot to ask. Other foster mothers had taken care of Nikki for me on many occasions. Still, I hesitated. I didn't think I ever wanted to hold another baby, even for a short time.

But the woman pleaded, "Please. I'm really tired, and Joe

doesn't take me out often. And Holly is a good baby. She'll probably sleep all the time I'm gone."

Reluctantly I took the infant seat from her. "She's part Black," the woman explained as I stroked one soft café-au-lait cheek and gazed at the soft brown eyes searching my own.

"She's so little," I commented.

"Two months," she smiled, "and just nine pounds. She started out at four." A car honked from the curb. "That's Joe," she explained. "I've got to go. Be back in a couple of hours."

Taking Holly from her infant seat, I sat in the rocker where I'd held Nikki so often. How comforting her small body felt. My arms ached with the relief of being able to love again, even if it was for just a few hours. Finally, smiling contentedly Holly drifted off into sleep, and I laid her in the crib that had once belonged to Nikki.

Hours passed. David and the children returned and peered with detached interest at the sleeping child. "She'll be here just a few hours," I assured David.

But Holly's foster mother did not return, and I finally changed Holly into a terry sleeper and gave her a bottle. She drank greedily and settled her head on my shoulder until sleep claimed her.

The rest of the family had gone to bed when the phone rang, "Hi, it's Karen," the voice began. "I was so tired that I had Joe bring me home. I'll pick up Holly in the morning."

Just what I needed—a two A.M. feeding. Besides Holly crowded my grief; she demanded to be fed, to be changed, and to be loved. "It's just overnight," I assured David, who surveyed me skeptically.

Small cooing sounds awoke me and for a moment I permitted myself to imagine it was Nikki. Finally I threw on my robe and picked up Holly, noting that it was 6 A.M. "You slept through the night." I smiled at her and was rewarded with a tentative grin.

After Holly had eaten, I propped her in her infant seat and began whipping some eggs for french toast for the rest of the family.

Matt, as usual, appeared first. "You're up," he commented with surprise.

"I had to feed Holly," I explained.

For a few moments that morning it seemed like old times—a family greedily devouring breakfast and a baby sitting in an infant seat occasionally giving a half-hearted kick with one leg. For a while I could pretend.

Karen did not call that day or the next, and when I tried to reach her there was no answer. "Thought she wasn't going to stay?" Lisa accused.

"She's not Nikki," Jill chimed in. "Nikki could talk and run and play, and this baby can't do anything."

"Nikki couldn't at first either," Lisa reminded her.

"She isn't staying; she already has a foster home and some day she'll be adopted," I assured them. I longed to go back to bed to hide out. But while Holly was here I could not.

At midmorning the phone rang. "It's Karen," a breathless voice greeted me. "I just called about Holly. Could you call Homes for Children and explain—you see, we're moving so I can't take Holly back after all."

And then she was gone. Muttering to myself, I looked under adoption agencies, found the number for Homes for Children, and dialed.

"Susan Lawrence," a voice greeted me cheerfully.

"You don't know me," I explained awkwardly, "but I have one of your babies."

She chuckled. "Let me guess. Karen moved again."

"This has happened before?" I asked incredulously.

"Let's just say it's not news. Well, how is Holly doing?"

We established that Holly was doing well although until that very moment I hadn't given a single thought to the fact that Holly was indeed settling in as though she owned the place. After chatting comfortably for a while, Susan commented, "It will be some time until Holly is placed for adoption. Since you already have a license and she's doing fine, I'd rather not move her again if you'd consider keeping her until I place her for adoption."

At that moment I couldn't think of a single reason Holly shouldn't stay until she was adopted. But after I'd hung up, I remembered that Holly would not permit me to lie on the bed and grieve all day.

David commented later with a sigh, "At least we know this one will go to a good home."

So Holly stayed and grew, a contented baby with a seemingly boundless amount of love to share. And gradually the children began to notice her and play with her and love her. Soon it was Holly's trills of laughter that filled the house.

In moments when Holly slept I began to commit the story of the child with faint footsteps to paper. And I began again to see the gift that Nikki had been to us, just borrowed, and for a brief time, but nonetheless a gift without measure.

And all those days Holly quietly and politely slipped into our hearts and lives. Perhaps because she was loved doubly, once for herself and once for Nikki, she grew into a thoroughly happy baby, at peace with herself and her world. For Holly there were no hidden terrors or curtained traumas. She recognized love as her own and claimed it fully.

Holly's birth mother did not decide to relinquish her for adoption until she was nearly a year old. And it was almost another whole year before the court freed her from her unknown father. In all those months Holly helped lift the burden of grief I had found too heavy to bear. And, of course, I came to love her deeply, as did David and the children.

And when the time came for Holly to be adopted, she was—by us. For as Susan, Holly's social worker, commented, "There was a plan in Holly's coming to you, but it wasn't mine. There were so many obstacles to freeing her for adoption." She giggled. "Those weren't my idea either. I can't explain Holly's placement rationally—the answers elude me. And I guess they should—the plan was greater than any of us."

Lynne, Susan's efficient secretary, brought in the placement papers, smiling broadly as David signed his name and took Holly from me while I scribbled my signature. As I took her back into my arms, Holly hugged me possessively, as if to say, "It takes grownups such a *very* long time to claim love."

Holly did not replace the child with faint footsteps; human beings are not interchangeable. Still it is strange that she has the same possessive hug and the same irrepressible giggle that Nikki had. I only know this much. In Matthew 11:28 Jesus tells us, "Come unto me all ye that labor and are heavy laden and I will give you rest." And in verse 30, "For my yoke is easy and my burden is light." I also know that in the moment when the pain was so great that I literally could not go on, Holly came for lunch and stayed to become our daughter. David and I and the children also know that "Every good and perfect gift is from above" (James 1:17). There knowledge ends and faith begins.

THROUGH DAVID'S PSALMS

Derek Prince

Derek Prince, internationally known Bible teacher and scholar, draws on his understanding of the Hebrew language and culture, and a comprehensive knowledge of Scripture, to present 101 meditations from the Psalms.
Each of these practical and enriching meditations is based on a specific passage and concludes with a faith response. They can be used either for personal meditation or for family devotions. They are intended for all those who want their lives enriched or who seek comfort and encouragement from the Scriptures.

LOVING GOD

Charles Colson

Loving God is the very purpose of the believer's life, the vocation for which he is made. However loving God is not easy and most people have given little real thought to what the greatest commandment really means.
Many books have been written on the individual subjects of repentence, Bible study, prayer, outreach, evangelism, holiness and other elements of the Christian life. In **Loving God**, Charles Colson draws all these elements together to look at the entire process of growing up as a Christian.
Combining vivid illustrations with straightforward exposition he shows how to live out the Christian faith in our daily lives. **Loving God** provides a real challenge to deeper commitment and points the way towards greater maturity.

OUT OF THE MELTING POT

Bob Gordon

Faith does not operate in a vacuum, it operates in human lives. God wants your life to be a crucible of faith.

Bob Gordon draws together Biblical principles and personal experience to provide valuable insights into this key area. Particular reference is made to the lessons he leant recently as God provided £600,000 to buy Roffey Place Christian Training Centre.

Out of the Melting Pot is Bob Gordon's powerful testimony to the work of God today and a profound challenge to shallow views of faith.

BILLY GRAHAM

John Pollock

By any reckoning, Billy Graham is one of the major religious figures of the twentieth-century.

John Pollock tells the highlights of the Billy Graham story briefly and vividly for the general reader. Using existing material and brand new information the story is taken right up the eve of Mission England.

This is an authoritative biography which pays special attention to the recent developments in Dr. Graham's life and ministry. Fully endorsed by Billy Graham himself, the book is full of fascinating new insights into the man and his mission.

". . . fascinating reading"

London Bible College Review

". . . a difficult book to put down"

Church of England Newspaper

THE TORN VEIL

Sister Gulshan and Thelma Sangster

Gulshan Fatima was brought up in a Muslim Sayed family according to the orthodox Islamic code of the Shias.

Suffering from a crippling paralysis she travelled to England in search of medical help. Although unsuccessful in medical terms, this trip marked the beginning of a spiritual awakening that led ultimately to her conversion to Christianity.

Gulshan and her father also travelled to Mecca in the hope that God would heal her, but that trip too was of no avail. However, Gulshan was not detered. She relentlessly pursued God and He faithfully answered her prayers. Her conversion, when it came, was dramatic and brought with a miraculous healing.

The Torn Veil is Sister Gulshan's thrilling testimony to the power of God which can break through every barrier.

NOW I CALL HIM BROTHER

Alec Smith

Alec Smith, son of Ian Smith the rebel Prime Minister of Rhodesia whose Unilateral Declaration of Independence plunged his country into twelve years of bloody racial war, has written his own story of those years.

The story of his life takes him from early years of rebellion against his role as 'Ian Smith's son' through his youth as a drop-out, hippy and drug peddler into the Rhodesian forces.

A dramatic Christian conversion experience at the height of the civil war transformed his life and led to the passionate conviction to see reconciliation and peace in a deeply divided country.

What follows is a thrilling account of how God can take a dedicated life and help to change the course of history.

If you wish to receive *regular information* about *new books*, please send your name and address to:

London Bible Warehouse
PO Box 123
Basingstoke
Hants RG23 7NL

Name...

Address..

....

....

....

I am especially interested in:
- ☐ Biographies
- ☐ Fiction
- ☐ Christian living
- ☐ Issue related books
- ☐ Academic books
- ☐ Bible study aids
- ☐ Children's books
- ☐ Music
- ☐ Other subjects

P.S. If you have ideas for new Christian Books or other products, please write to us too!